D1629600

The Just Enterprise

By the same author

The Future of Private Enterprise
The People's Church
The Responsible Company
The Responsible Worker

The Just Enterprise

GEORGE GOYDER CBE

Author of *The Responsible Company*

Foreword by Sir Peter Parker

ANDRE DEUTSCH

For My Children and Grandchildren

First published in 1987 by
André Deutsch Limited
105–106 Great Russell Street London WC1B 3LJ

British Library Cataloguing in Publication Data

Goyder, G.E.
The just enterprise.
1. Corporation law – Great Britain
I. Title
344.106'66 KD2079

ISBN 0 233 98157 8

Typeset by Setrite Typesetters Limited
Printed in Great Britain by
Ebenezer Baylis & Son Ltd Worcester

CONTENTS

The problem is to find some principle of
justice upon which human association for the
production of wealth can be founded.

R.H. Tawney: Commonplace Book for 8 January 1914.

If England is to continue free, she must rest
upon the intermediate institutions.

Sir Arthur Bryant: *English Saga*, 1940, p. 186.

ACKNOWLEDGEMENTS

In writing this book I have had the invaluable encouragement of friends, among whom I should especially mention Philip Sadler CBE, Principal of Ashridge Management College; Lord Young of Dartington; Professor L.C.B. Gower; Peter Thompson; John Garnett CBE; and Sir Peter Parker, who has been so kind as to write the Foreword. The members of my family have borne my preoccupation with *The Just Enterprise* for several years and have made excellent criticisms and suggestions, particularly my son Mark. Having said this, I should add that I alone am responsible for any errors or omissions in the text.

I would like to thank Eileen Gough and Jill Dyer for typing the manuscript, and my publisher André Deutsch and his colleagues for their helpfulness. Finally, I acknowledge with gratitude the endless patience and constant support of my wife. She has taught me that marriage is nature's own just enterprise. In the words of Sir Thomas Browne: 'When Industry builds on Nature we may expect Pyramids.'

George Goyder, March 1987

FOREWORD

Make a brave assumption: that most men and women at work – at any level in the organisation, on the floor or in the field, or in the boardroom – want to be responsible. I take that optimistic premise to be self-evident in the vitality of any successful enterprise. But responsible to whom? That is the question and it lies at the troubled heart of our industrial democracy. The question takes many forms. Why should anyone obey an order? Where does sovereignty lie? What are the just rewards of responsibility? What are the balances of individual freedom and social responsibility? Of course, the question has begged its way through centuries, long before democracy and industrialisation. It is the pursuit of justice, and that is a show that has and will run and run. With the barbaric triumph of the steam engine and steel, the challenge gained new power. The old patterns of society were disrupted. How are we to establish the balance of justice in industrial democracy? Not without difficulty, and not without giving much more attention to that special agent of change, the producer of wealth in modern society: the company. George Goyder describes it as 'the decisive economic influence of our time', yet, as he demonstrates so clearly, its objectives and its constitution are maddeningly out of date.

Can it be just, for instance, that a lifelong employee is not a member of the company – that only as a shareholder with equity he can be that? The word equity jars in this context. We shall have to do better than this, in fairness, both in modern enterprise and in our society. In fact, company law lags behind the reality of the best practice. Not surprisingly, the basic concepts of its constitution were born at the start of our industrial revolution, when the family was still the unit of responsibility.

The mid-Victorian codification of limited liability transformed the scope of responsibility and risk-taking: it was the birth certificate of the entrepreneur. What a change there has been since then, and above all in two ways. Firstly, the decisive corporations take their giant strides easily about the global market-place: high-tech flies over fading frontier signs; night does not follow day in twenty-four-hour financial services. Secondly, today's democracy insists that a citizen has a share in what goes on, and has a right to speak and ask about what concerns him or her. It is the reconciliation of efficiency and citizenship that challenges us. But it is not a romantic notion. Many companies of excellence, here and in other countries, have attempted it already, as George Goyder describes. Such companies as Sears Roebuck, Marks & Spencer, Shell, and, as early as 1896, Zeiss, have endeavoured to give workers a vested interest in the performance of their organization. Among the pace-makers of profitability, social responsibility of enterprise is no longer left to the last gasped paragraph of the chairman's statement where the board thanks the workers – the maraschino cherry popped onto the grapefruit. Social policy is inseparable from long-term success.

This means more than consultation within the working community, more than wider shareownership; vital and discernible as both are. They are internal priorities. What matters now is a balance of interests and responsibilities between the company, its employees, the local community, the government, and, as Goyder puts it, above all the customers who no longer enjoy the protection of a free competitive market economy à la Adam Smith.

With judo-like skill George Goyder takes the force of Adam Smith and turns it to his own case for reform. Adam Smith, after all, foresaw the stupefying, soul-boggling effects on the worker of the progress of division of labour. He was a moral philosopher as well as an economist: 'All the members of a balanced society stand in need of each other's assistance ... where the necessary assistance is reciprocally afforded ... the society flourished and is happy.' Adam Smith was a believer in natural justice. Were he alive today, Goyder argues, he would be applying the law of human mutuality both in legal and organisational terms, pressing for action against monopolies and price rings, for customer protection and in favour of the limitation of dividends. Certainly he would be anatomising the power and performance of the great international corporations. He would be striving to redesign the company to make it more effective and just.

George Goyder, also a believer in natural justice, strives towards that vision of the unity of industrial and social purposes. *The Future of Private Enterprise* (1951), *The Responsible Company* (1961), *The Responsible Worker* (1975), all bear witness to the vision that has not failed him. The same vision guided his business career, in his long-term role as chief British executive of the International Paper Company of the United States and Canada; during wartime he even undertook the hazardous job of being just to the newspaper proprietors of Great Britain in the rationing of newsprint. In this book he earths the vision in his specific series of reforms of company law and organisation.

These call for changes in company law in the light of a new realism in business: that it should reflect the multiple interests at stake within any enterprise; that it should establish a juster balance than the present law allows between shareholders, employees, society and customers. Without such explicit definition, business is left with a cat's cradle of contrary commitments. With it we can make real the new relationship of profits and trust that high-tech democracy demands.

The Just Enterprise has the courage to define these problems in practical detail and an original programme of change.

George Goyder himself is an original. He is crammed with scholarship, experience, hope and surprise. He is a businessman and a seer, a worker and a doer, an efficient man for whom efficiency is simply not enough. He is a Christian and a radical and (not at all incidentally) the founder, with Sir Geoffrey Keynes, of the William Blake Trust. He is also a whistle-blower. In this fine work he moves onto the muddy field where capital and labour have played their ideological games for so long. And he advances from there with new ideas and scope which should command the attention of the businessman and the trade unionist, the statesman and the citizen.

PREFACE

Today, in the large company, social responsibility is accepted as a significant aspect of corporate behaviour. In the USA many large companies have a department of social responsibility, while it has become a commonplace of management teaching that productivity is increased when an organisation behaves in a socially responsible manner. Far from judicious expenditure on social objectives being any disadvantage to the shareholders, it has been realised that in the long run the company depends on the goodwill of those it serves, including the community of which it is a member.

There is, however, another way of looking at the question of social responsibility. This sees the company not just as an instrument for maximising profit in the interest of shareholders, but as a wealth-creating organism in the service of the consumers, employees and the community as well as of the shareholders. This raises a problem of the first magnitude. For, in the words of the historian Sir Arthur Bryant,

> A limited liability company has no conscience. A priesthood of figures cannot consider claims of morality and justice that conflict with its mathematical formulas; it must live by its own rules. Man, who once tried to model his life on the divine, came to take his orders from the lender of money and the chartered accountant acting in their purely professional capacity. It is not the profit motive which is to blame. Free men have at all times sought profit from their labour. It is its enthronement to the exclusion of other motives far more important.[1]

Today the question to be asked of every political programme and economic activity is not only 'will it pay?' but 'will it make better men and women?' The survival of democracy requires the building up of the intermediate associations between the individual and the state, of which the most important are the family and the company. This book deals with the latter. It is written in the belief that the problems created by an industrial civilisation – bad housing, rundown services, inner-city dereliction, low morale and massive unemployment – demand a wider and longer view than immediate profit from the business community. The time has come to bring in the responsible company,[2] based on an industrial philosophy which, like that propounded by Adam Smith in *The Wealth of Nations,* looks to justice; but a form of justice consistent with the needs of the twenty-first rather than the eighteenth century.

PART 1

THE PROBLEM

1
Towards a Fresh Philosophy of Enterprise

We need a fresh vision of business enterprise. In a society that has become predominantly urban and suburban we need a form of work organisation, and a work ethic, that offer men and women a certain scope, a certain dignity and freedom, and not just an existence.

Today a hundred firms account for one half of the country's manufactures. They in turn control thousands of smaller concerns which depend upon them for orders. A survey by the Institute of Economic Affairs, as long ago as 1959, showed 134 British companies owning 2,686 subsidiaries. A single motor manufacturer will control hundreds of dealers, an oil company thousands of filling stations. Toyota in Japan has over 140 major suppliers employing some 40,000 sub-contractors.

In an industrialised society the most important of all productive organisations is the company, which dominates the life of the country by being the focus of its work and service. It is in the company that men must be able to feel free if democracy is to survive. And this means redesigning the company to express the need of ordinary people for a worthwhile purpose in their work and equality in pursuing it.

We are inclined to regard the role of the law as negative, because its method is to prohibit what society regards as anti-social. But the purpose, as distinct from the method of the law, is positive. The law sets the guidelines for society. It marks out the rights of individuals and reconciles conflicting claims. In today's conditions we need a law which will define the social responsibilities of the great industrial and commercial concerns which have come to dominate the economic life of advanced industrial countries like Britain. It must be a *company* law, because it is the company which is the dominant economic influence in our time. We might expect company law in Britain and the United States to have been modified to take account of the social changes in these countries during the past thirty years. If so, we should be disappointed. Company law in Britain (and in the USA) is in many essential respects the same as when it was first enacted over a century ago, when the welfare state was unknown, before the rise of the multinational or nationalised company, and before the development of private corporations exercising public monopoly, like British Gas, or of giant quasi-monopolies like British Telecom and the oil companies. The company law we have today was also formulated before the rise to power of the trades unions. All these social developments have gone almost unnoticed by company law.

When limited liability was first enacted in 1855 and consolidated in the Companies Act of 1862, British industry was controlled by the individual proprietors of a very large number of small family enterprises. Before the Act of 1855 the proprietor of a business stood to lose all he possessed if his business became insolvent, and his partner or backer likewise. Only after 1855 did limited liability make it practically possible for a company to grow indefinitely, until we come to the position today, when a small group of men exercise control over commercial empires that are richer than many sovereign states. The size and scale of industrial organisation has altered out of recognition since the invention of limited liability one hundred and more years ago. But in that time virtually nothing has been done to bring company law into line with social reality.

This is what puts the future of democracy in doubt, given the dominant role of business in the life of the community and its involvement in every aspect of our lives; where we live, how and when we work, and for what objectives. What can the worker (to be taken hereafter as referring both to men and women) expect from his job? Can he expect to find in it emotional security, as the result of a worthwhile and satisfying purpose shared between a group of likeminded people? What can redeem the boredom of so much work in an industrial age? The technology of large-scale production denies to many a worker the kind of work he most enjoys – personal, creative, whole, useful work – and gives him instead work of a fragmented kind, seemingly without purpose, which he does not enjoy at all. When dockers and printers earning more than teachers and parsons engage in a battle of wits and nerves by striking against the enterprise that provides them with their livelihood, who can say what deep-seated malaise lies at the root of their corporately expressed dissatisfaction? The fact that the most intransigent strikes occur among the highest-paid workers – miners, dockers and printers – points to the fact that men need more than high wages. Their real underlying need is for emotional security and a sense of purpose in their work. If this is true, we must ask how a sense of purpose and emotional assent can be given to the workers, in addition to fair wages. What kind of a company will best attract the loyalty of its employees?

When the battle for a more acceptable form of work organisation than the limited liability company at present provides is taken into party politics, the truth is in danger of being lost in a war of words. *The Oxford English Dictionary* defines capitalism as 'the condition of possessing capital, a system which favours the existence of people who have capital available for employment in reproductive enterprise.' Since under any political system the provision of capital depends on its prior creation, we are all capitalists of a kind. But in a democracy there must also be a concern for the social values of justice, equality and moderation, and all who cherish and practise these values are in some degree socialists. To reconcile these complementary aims we need in industry a framework of law which is able to command the confidence of employees, financial backers, customers and the community at large. The creation of a sense of partnership in industry and commerce is the most urgent task facing us in domestic politics.

What has gone wrong with company law? Principally, that it fails to state what the purpose of a company is. It gives to the directors, as agents of the shareholders, *de facto* control of the company's policy and to the other interests – such as the workers' – no corresponding rights. Unlike previous forms of work organisation, of which the fifteenth-century guilds and the chartered corporations which followed them were typical, a limited liability company is not constitutionally concerned with quality or value, or with the public interest. In the light of the commanding power which the large company today exercises in the economy, the law governing it in Britain has become a defective instrument for controlling industry. Our political system has come increasingly to reflect the conflict of purpose inherent in existing company law by identifying the Conservative and Labour parties each with vested interests, respectively that of capital and labour, both of which, together with the invaluable heritage of the Liberal tradition, must in the end be reconciled within the framework of the individual company. A cycle of government alternating between parties with inconsistent ideologies does not lend itself to the continuity of policy which business planning requires. Spasmodic government intervention in the larger company is as debilitating to management as it is self-defeating. What is needed is to bring company law into line with the broadest possible spectrum of public opinion and social policy, and then to leave the company free to follow its own aims. Our failure to make company law express in its structure and mode of operation that concern for moderation, equality and justice upon which democracy itself depends is a failure of will. The reconciliation of authority and liberty in industry and commerce must follow the path of seeking to do justice to all the constituent elements *within* the structure of the individual company.

The challenge we face is to discover a philosophy of company law which is socially and morally acceptable and at the same time encourages efficiency. We need to apply the principle of trusteeship, which is an expression of the natural law. As we shall see in Chapter 4, economists have tended to overlook the fact that Adam Smith was a natural law philosopher, and *The Wealth of Nations* rooted in natural law thinking. We have to return to the mode of thought which asks how public policy can best harness economic initiative so as to bring about a harmony of interest in the community with expansion that is not socially divisive.

Industrialism imposes great strains on human beings, as we shall see in the following chapters. The division of labour required by mass-production breaks work up into segments. Splitting work into small segments reduces the capacity of the worker to understand its purpose, while the concentration of large numbers of men and women in factories limits their exercise of personal responsibility. Unless a way can be found to give back to the worker what he lost with the coming of the industrial revolution, namely the ownership of his work, the prospect for the survival of democracy appears distinctly unfavourable. Whereas despotisms are maintained through fear, and monarchies and aristocracies through honour and the laws, the survival of democracy depends upon something more difficult: virtue in the citizen.[1] By virtue Montesquieu understood love of country, love of equality, and moderation: 'Democracy has two excesses to avoid, the spirit of inequality which leads to aristocracy or monarchy; and the spirit of extreme equality, which leads to despotic power.'[2]

In an industrialised society – and Britain is among the most industrialised nations in the world, with only two per cent of its people living and working on the land – personal responsibility in large enterprise will remain at a discount so long as industry is permanently controlled by the agents of outside interests, whether those interests be private shareholders or a government department. What the individual worker seeks is the ownership of his work, with the security that goes with it. If he cannot acquire a sense of belonging through the company for which he works, he will seek to acquire it through his trade union, and the union will seek to acquire it for its members through political action.

The introduction in Britain after the 1939–45 war of a welfare state, with full employment which lasted for nearly a generation, enabled the workers through their trades unions to raise their sights in the knowledge that, when faced by ill-health, old age, poverty or unemployment, they would be protected. This knowledge gave the workers a freedom from fear which encouraged them to make unprecedented demands through their unions. The creation of monopolies in the basic industries of coal, gas, steel, docks and railways, under the government's nationalisation programme, contributed to the continuous upward pressure on wages, as did the spate of takeover bids that accompanied the period of post-war prosperity. This added still further to the power of organised labour and enabled it to press continously for better conditions and higher pay. Economists differ as to whether the resulting wage demands were the main cause of the inflation that followed, but there can be no doubt that they were a contributory factor. The result of thirty years of rising expectations had been to create demands that could be realised only through a radical change in the attitude to work. In a democratic and welfare society, efficiency can be maximised only when the positive energies of ordinary men and women are engaged. The reservoir of productivity latent in human attitudes is possibly our greatest untapped resource.

Because the power and influence of the large company now spreads right through the economy, the company has taken on many of the characteristics of a trust; that is to say, it now stands in a relationship of trust to government, the local community, shareholders, employees, and above all to its customers, who no longer necessarily enjoy the protection of a free and competitive market economy as intended by Adam Smith.

In his classic review of the legal institutions of the ancient world, Sir Henry Maine shows that the happiness of a people depends on the promptitude with which the law is changed to accord with social necessities. In looking at the political lessons to be learnt from our forebears, Maine concluded that the glory that was ancient Greece in the fourth and fifth centuries BC was made possible by Solon's legislation a century earlier. In the same way, Rome achieved the zenith of its power following the promulgation of the law of the Twelve Tables, while the expansion of Israel followed the gift of the Ten Commandments. Except for the last, none of these codes was complete or systematic. But each made public an expression of social purpose in terms that decisively influenced the growth of a civilisation. 'The point on which turned the history of the race was, at what point, at what stage of their social progress, they should have their laws put into writing.'[3]

Today we face the same necessity for a forward looking restatement of the law governing the company, especially the public company employing large numbers of people. We have to provide the company with a legal purpose that is consistent with its actual development. This means a company with whose purposes the employee can be at home. It means a company which the consumer can trust. It means a company which seeks to act as a responsible member of the community of which it is a member and one that can be called to account when there is gross failure to act justly. It means legislating for the responsible company.

The chapters which follow aim to show how the responsible company can be brought into being through the constructive use of the law, backed by a social opinion that is well ahead of the law. We cannot turn the clock back, but we can set the clock right by turning it forward. In the words of Lord Eustace Percy:

> Here is the most urgent challenge to political invention ever offered to the jurist and the statesman. The human association which in fact produces and distributes wealth, the association of workmen, managers, technicians and directors, is not an association recognised by the law. The association which the law does recognise – the association of shareholders, creditors and directors – is incapable of production or distribution and is not expected by the law to perform these functions. We have to give law to the real association and to withdraw meaningless privilege from the imaginary one.[4]

If that challenge seemed urgent when it was uttered in 1944, how much more urgent is it today!

2
Minimising the Human Cost of Industrialism

In the West, as in the East, the economic, and therefore the social, basis of society has from time immemorial been agriculture. An industrial society is a relatively new phenomenon, dating from the industrial revolution which began in Britain during the last quarter of the eighteenth century, just two hundred years ago. The consequences of this revolution for people at work have been far-reaching. On the one hand the individual worker's lot has improved in respect of his standard of living, mobility, expectation of life and general welfare. But with these gains have gone corresponding losses. In traditional agricultural society the worker had a settled role, and the standing that went with it, whether as tenant, freeholder, or serf. By removing production from the farm and village to the factory and town the industrial revolution brought about the dissolution of these ties. The worker became a hand, without certainty of occupation or security of tenure. He suffered not only from the risk of being unemployed, but also from the emotional insecurity of no longer belonging to a society in which he had a settled and assured role. It is this change in the status of the worker that has created so much dissatisfaction in our time. As Peter Laslett, the social historian, writes:

> The ending of the system which ensured that however he was paid, however little he owned, or however close he was to the point of starvation, a man usually lived and worked within the family, the circle of affection, released enough dissatisfaction to account for all the restlessness which has marked the progress of the industrial world.[1]

As a result of the industrial revolution, work has changed its nature. In traditional agriculture the worker followed the seasons of the year and they created the rhythm that governed his work.

But in the factory and office the rhythm of work is man-made, while the division of labour results in the worker doing only a small fraction of a total task. As a result the worker has become dependent on the will of management rather than upon the weather. It makes a profound difference to one's attitude to work. What is acceptable when imposed by nature can seem unacceptable coming from one's fellow man.

The fact that the industrial revolution was also a technological revolution, and that changes in technology have been continuous as a result of man's inventiveness, combined with international competition, imposes a further strain on the worker: that of being required to adapt continuously to altered working conditions. This again makes for uncertainty and, with uncertainty, resistance. Small wonder that powerful trades unions have grown up with the object of defending the worker from unreasonable change and from exploitation as a human being.

In the trade union movement of Britain we have inherited a special legacy of distrust of the employer: not of individual or single employers, but of employers in general. We are face to face with a collective conscience created by generations of experience, often bitter and inhuman. This collective experience dictates the inherited mythology which still animates the mind of the trade union movement as a corporate body. Corporate bodies do not act like their individual members, but in response to a group purpose forged by generations – seven generations in this case – of collective experience, moulded by the harsh conditions of factory employment and personal insecurity so well described by the Hammonds,[2] and continuing down to the present day. This is the legacy of industrialisation in its first phase and one which we ignore at our peril, whether as statesmen or businessmen. It finds expression in a novel written in 1866.

> It isn't a man's share just to mind your pin-making, or your glass blowing, and higgle about your own wages, and bring up your family to be ignorant sons of ignorant fathers, and no better prospect; that's a slave's share; we want a free-man's share, and that is to think and speak and act about what concerns us all.[3]

The inhuman consequences of the division of labour brought about by the industrial revolution were anticipated by Adam Smith in *The Wealth of Nations*, where he writes:

> In the progress of the division of labour, the employment of the far greater part of those who live by labour ... comes to be confined to a

few very simple operations; frequently to one or two . . . the man whose whole life is spent in performing a few simple operations . . . has no occasion to exercise his understanding . . . he naturally loses, therefore, the habit of such exertion, and generally becomes as stupid and ignorant as it is possible for a human being to become. The torpor of his mind renders him not only incapable of relishing or bearing a part in any rational conversation, but of conceiving any generous, noble, or tender sentiment, and consequently of forming any just judgment concerning many even of the ordinary duties of private life.[4]

In an industrial as opposed to an agricultural society, a man is known by what he does rather than by what he is. When we introduce two people today almost the first question asked is: 'What do you do?' This is because we need to relate the person to our own working experience. It is our work that gives us social significance. To have to reply 'Nothing' is a declaration of social irrelevance. It means that the speaker, however temporarily, has lost his place in society. And this is to put one's personality in jeopardy, for personality grows by relationship.* A developed system of social welfare may cushion the blow economically for a time, but it cannot replace the social satisfaction that work, even unpleasant work, brings with it through association. Not to be able to contribute by work to the society of which one is a member, is to put a premium on crime as an alternative way of life; the steady increase of criminality in an industrial society which is failing to provide employment, let alone satisfying employment, seems inevitable.

The problem created by the fully industrialised society, which Britain is one of the first countries to experience, is a problem of reconciling the needs of the worker for personal, creative, useful and whole work which he can enjoy, with the scale of production demanded by an advanced technology. The answer, looking to the future, may lie with the micro-processor and computer, by taking the drudgery out of work and reducing the need for human oversight when applied to manufacturing industry. It is too early to say what the net effect will be on employment, but a pointer is the rapid growth in employment in the service sector in the USA, from one-third to two-thirds of the working population between 1960 and 1980. What can be stated with certainty

* The word 'person' comes from *persona*, the mask worn by a player on the classical stage.

is that once industry can no longer provide sufficient employment for the workforce (directly or indirectly), and agriculture in its modern mechanised form no longer provides an alternative, the end of industrialism will have been reached, so far as Adam Smith's vision goes. A new era will have dawned in which employment will have become as important as production, and human satisfaction as important as technology.

For Britain this moment has arrived. The first industrial revolution is over, and what will replace it has yet to be devised. We know it will be different. We can be sure it will make great demands, particularly from the company as the prevailing work form. Whatever its exact legal status, the company of the future will be required to pay attention to the welfare of the people it employs as much as to the quality of its products, and to the environment of which it is a part, as well as to the capital invested in the business. This is the task of a company pursuing a balance between economic performance and social welfare, or, in other words, a responsible company.

The company of the future will have to learn the technique of balancing and optimising the claims made upon it. These claims come from a variety of sources – customers, workers, locality, government, shareholders – whose interests have to be reconciled, not once and for all, but from day to day. When we regard company policy in the light of balancing claims, we are in fact invoking the principle of justice as the basis of policy in a company. That principle, by whatever verbal jargon we choose to conceal it – self-interest, necessity, social responsibility, the pursuit of corporate goals – is the principle of balance.

The balanced company is one which seeks continuously to act with justice towards those it serves, including its workforce and customers. Since justice, like charity, begins at home, the first consideration of a company's management must be the maintenance of profitability, just as health comes first for the individual. We have to meet our own basic needs before we can meet the needs of others. But when this has been said we have only begun to face the claims of justice upon the company. If the human cost of industrialism is to be minimised, we must abandon the attitude of indifference to the social conditions of work which characterised the Victorian era.

The worker's safety, housing, transport, environment and, above all, his opportunities to grow as an individual through his work are all necessary areas of concern to the responsible company. But they do not justify the company invading the private life of the worker, or attempting to influence what he does out of the office or workshop. Paternalism and indifference have equally to be shunned.

3
The Metamorphosis of the Company

The word 'company' may be used to describe any association of people engaged in a common task.* The earliest companies consisted of families, and the expression 'keeping company' is still sometimes used of a couple contemplating marriage. They are said to form a 'partnership', and partnership and company are words used to describe the two main types of organisation for carrying on a business recognised by the law of England. But while the partnership has remained substantially in its original form of a group of people sharing risks, the company has been totally metamorphosed until it has become the predominant economic institution of the West. General Motors is such a company, with assets which exceed the wealth of all but the largest nation states.

This transition from family-controlled business to giant corporation was made possible by the invention of limited liability in the middle of the nineteenth century. The moving spirit was Robert Lowe, Vice-President of the Board of Trade (afterwards Lord Sherbrooke) whose 'elegant but imprudent leadership' brought about the defeat of Gladstone's Reform Bill in 1866 and the resignation of the government. Lowe was a controversial figure and his innovation offended the business community of Manchester, who thought it would prove subversive to the moral responsibility of businessmen. In retrospect we can see that the invention of limited liability was of crucial importance to the second phase of the industrial revolution which began about 1850. Joined with the technology of mass production, and the growing resources of a centralised financial system based on

* Company: either from *con* and *pagus*, one of the same town; or *con panis*, one that eats of the same mess. *Dr Johnson's Dictionary*.

the City of London, it removed the barriers which had previously tied the entrepreneur to a small-scale operation. The limiting factor had been the risk entailed by unlimited liability. Failure could not only bankrupt the owner of a business but reduce to penury his entire family and any friends who might have supported him.

This actually happened to Sir Walter Scott. In 1809 Sir Walter had underwritten his publisher Ballantyne, as an act of friendship rather than as an investment. Suddenly in 1825 he found himself liable for a debt of £130,000, an enormous sum in those days. How Sir Walter bravely struggled to pay off this great sum by writing the novels that have made him famous, is a matter of history and tragedy. It could have happened to anyone who invested in a family business before the invention of limited liability and it was this as much as poor transport facilities that kept business small in scale. Small was not only beautiful; it was safe. But once a company could borrow all the money it needed to expand without unlimited personal liability falling on directors or shareholders, there was no longer any limit to the size to which the company might grow.

The rate of industrialisation could now proceed at breakneck speed until Britain became the first fully industrialised nation in history. The method used was to sell shares to the public, who invested in the hope of gaining a profit but in the knowledge that they might lose their stake if the company failed. That stake was, however, the full extent of the shareholders' liability.

We will return to the social consequences of limited liability. But we must now ask 'What is the purpose of a company?' Put most simply, a company exists to produce goods and services for its customers. In a society of competing companies, failure to meet the needs of the customer leads to liquidation. In a free society the consumer is king, and business exists to satisfy his needs. But, as Kenneth Galbraith[1] has pointed out, we no longer live in the kind of free society which Adam Smith envisaged, consisting of a large number of small competing firms in a local market. Many of the big companies have grown into oligopolies, influencing by their advertising and market dominance the demand for their products and services. For example, a few large companies that manufacture electric light bulbs are said to do so to an agreed specification which ensures that they (the bulbs, not the companies) do not last too long. But the misuse of corporate producer power leads to its antidote; the rise of an independent consumer movement, becoming increasingly powerful in the USA through the efforts of Ralph Nader, and of Michael (now Lord) Young in Britain, founder of the Consumers' Association, publishers of *Which*?

Although the company serves the consumer and depends upon his custom, company law does not require the directors to exercise any particular care for the interests of its customers. Such consumer protection as exists has been achieved by legislation in specific areas such as product liability. In this the company differs from the mediaeval guild where quality control and craftsmanship were prime objects of the company itself. The same is true of the company's present relationship with the community. Company law lays no responsibility upon the directors to see that the company behaves in a socially responsible manner. The company is generally thought of (wrongly, as we shall see) as the creature of its shareholders; the successors of the men and women who subscribed the initial capital and put their signature to the memorandum and articles: the documents setting out the formal purposes of the company and its internal regulations. Nothing need be, nor generally is, said about the company's duties to its employees, customers or the community. In this, modern company law differs profoundly from the guilds and chartered companies which preceded it. For

> the essential function of these craft corporations [in 1650] was to assume responsibility for the practice of their trades in matters such as workmanship, quality and fair dealing . . . So far the element of capital had not made an appearance, it had existed in the small funds accumulated by master craftsmen, perhaps out of their savings as journeymen, to enable them to rent a house and buy the tools and materials necessary to set up in business for themselves. But the chief elements in these new business enterprises were the skill and connection of the craftsman. The quality of his goods and his reputation had to be established; his fund must carry him over the period of establishment. This was broadly the limit of the function of capital in the time of the guilds.[2]

In the seventeeth and eighteenth centuries, after the collapse of the guilds, the first essential of a company's existence was that it should serve a public purpose. The grant of incorporation was not a grant for private gain but for the public benefit. Incorporation was granted by act of parliament, and it was against the abuse of this monopoly power that Adam Smith wrote. It was not until the middle of the nineteenth century that any body of seven or more persons could apply for corporate status, with the privileges of perpetual succession and limited liability, when company law took the general form that it has to the present day.

Who are the owners of a modern company? Certainly not the employees; for they are hardly mentioned in company law. Company chairmen frequently refer at the annual shareholders' meeting to 'your company' as if the shareholders were jointly the owners of the company. But this is not strictly correct. In law the company is a distinct corporate entity with a separate personality governed by its declaration of purpose and established by the fact of its incorporation.

From time immemorial the corporation has been distinguished in English law from its members. According to C.A. Cooke (*Corporation, Trust & Company*, page 176), the most interesting piece of new company law after the Act of 1862 is the decision in *Salomon v Salomon & Co.* (1897) which established the principle that a corporation is something different from its members, a judgement repeated in 1947, when in *Short v Treasury Commissioners* Lord Justice Evershed, summing up, said, 'shareholders are not in the eye of the law part owners of the undertaking. The undertaking is something different from the totality of its shareholdings.' In 1943 the government had taken over Short Brothers as a wartime measure and offered the shareholders the then stock exchange value of the shares, which had fallen heavily on the news of the takeover. The shareholders' auditors valued the company's net assets and they were found to be worth fifty per cent more than the offer. But the courts held that the shareholders were not entitled to the company's net realisable asset value because they did not own the company and it had not been liquidated.[3] The principle that a company is a separate entity and is not ownable by its shareholders applies also in Canadian and US law, as it does in Sweden and West Germany.

It is worth pausing to consider for a moment the underlying meaning of the word 'own'. We think of it in terms of rights. If I own a house, that means I have a *right* to live in it or to dispose of it. But the word used for possession from the fourteenth to the seventeenth century was not 'own' but 'owe'. Before me as I write lies a manuscript copy of John Wycliffe's *New Testament*. At the side of the page is written 'John Shaw oweth this book.' (Sir John Shaw was Lord Mayor of London in 1501.) Many similar illustrations could be given of the fact that ownership was originally 'owership'. The obligations of a company, what it 'owes', as distinct from what it owns, embraces its duties not only to its shareholders, but also to its employees, consumers, and the community of which the company forms a part.

The distinction between a company and its shareholders is 'a fundamental or cardinal distinction – a distinction which must be firmly grasped,' says Palmer in the 17th edition of his standard work on company law.[4] How has it come about that a distinction so important should have been overlooked for so long? For an answer we must look at the way in which companies developed after the invention of limited liability. At first they were family affairs, and in the family the head is responsible for the whole. Before the invention of limited liability the proprietor could well talk of being the 'owner' of his family firm. After he had incorporated the business under the new law in order to take advantage of limited liability, at first nothing would appear to have changed. The same people would continue to act in the same way. So it was natural to continue to speak of the company as if it were the proprietor's 'own'. It was the gradual transition from a domestic to a factory-based system of industry that made 'ownership' separate from control. For so long as the proprietor and his family owned all the shares in the new limited liability company they still could reasonably, if not quite accurately, talk of owning the firm. But this ceased to be the case when the company grew into a public joint stock company with its shares quoted on the Stock Exchange. Now it was no longer the proprietor who controlled the company but a group of people called the shareholders, who might bear no relationship to one another except their desire for profit, and no sense of obligation either to the company's employees or to the community in which it operated. This divorce of ownership (or owership) from responsibility was to become complete with the advent of the national and multinational company in the twentieth century.

What the worker lost as a result of the industrial revolution was his sense of security. In the time of the guilds he had been a partner in a joint enterprise. Then, as the guilds broke up and private capital took over, he might still work in a family firm whose proprietor was a relative or neighbour. With the industrial revolution came the need to herd the workforce into factories, where, as a result of the growing division of labour, they first lost control of the product, then of the company, and finally of the job. The transition from being a skilled craftsman to being a hand in a factory was bad enough. It was made worse by the exclusion of the employees from any legal rights within the organisation to which they gave the best years of their lives. As Peter Laslett has written, 'Time was when the whole of life went forward in the family, in a circle of loved, familiar faces, known and fondled objects, all to human size. That time has gone forever. It makes us very different from our ancestors.'[5]

However large it may have become, the company can still be returned to its origins as a family at work. Size does not make humanity impossible, provided the separate units are small. The church is an example of an organisation which has retained its ability to speak to and for the individual. The Church of England is a company of some 2½ million members who belong to over 12,000 separate congregations, of an average size of two hundred people, each taking its share of responsibility for its services. In contrast, we see that the industrial and commercial company, as it has grown in size, has been allowed to shed its social responsibilities and to reduce the position of the employees until they have no status as members. (But see page 54 for the effect of the 1985 Companies Act.) The task before us is to reconstruct the law of the limited liability company. It is absurd that a law designed for family business a century ago should continue to apply, without substantial change, to the whole of industry today regardless of the size and purpose of the company. This represents the abdication of the state from its responsibility to create responsible institutions.

One of the earliest sociologists, Emile Durkheim,[6] foresaw the need for moral regulation in industry. 'The corporations', wrote Durkheim, 'will establish and sanction the ethics appropriate to each occupational category, and provide a focus for the moral consciousness of the workers within that category. In a general way, they will resemble the mediaeval guilds, but without manifesting the same inflexible and re-actionary character.' This was written in 1893, when the industrial revolution was still in an early stage. Durkheim had already realised that this was not a task the trades unions could possibly fulfil, and the reason he gives holds good today: 'The trade unions are primarily bodies organised with the sole object of furthering the interests of their members.'

It is unrealistic to think that by some sudden enlightenment the trade union movement will change its purpose and direction.

This is an illusion. It is not by this means that reform will come about. It is to the rectification of the law and practice of the company as the repository of social justice in the creation of wealth that we must look; not to the body which has arisen as a protest against the injustice of company law. The role of protest and the role of creation are distinct roles. When the company conforms to social justice, and not before, the trades unions will begin to change and look with different eyes at their role. The essential reform is institutional – the bringing into being of the responsible company.

It is not as if shareholders in public companies have fared particularly well in recent years. According to the Royal Commission on the Distribution of Income and Wealth,[7] British shareholders' average return in dividends, after allowing for taxation and inflation, was 2.6 per cent per annum between 1948 and 1974,* and similar figures have been quoted for the same period in the USA.[8] This reflects the growing power of the trades unions in a welfare economy, enabling them to reduce the real return on equity investments to a level where it is no longer attractive to the private investor. So long as employees have neither a stake in the enterprise nor any part in the formulation of corporate policy, it is hardly surprising that their unions should press their claims to the limit, regardless of the long-term effects on capital investment. What is required is an incentive for employees to take the long view of the company and its need for regular capital formation. As it is, the men see the company's shareholders exercising rights of control in perpetuity in an enterprise which extinguishes the workers' rights upon retirement or death.

It is this discrepancy in time between the reward of capital and of work which has alienated the unions and the men and women they represent. It is not the size of the dividend but its perpetual nature and its claim to confer a permanent right to exclusive control that is usurious and has created a sense of grievance which puts the future of the company in its present form into doubt.

We shall see, in the next chapter, that if Adam Smith were alive, he would be an advocate of company law reform rather

* To dividends on shares must be added capital gains. In the absence of official figures, it must be assumed that in 1975–1985 these were substantial. However, capital gains may at any time become capital losses.

than relying upon the 'invisible hand'. Nor would Smith be satisfied with the way privatisation of monopolies has been carried out by the Conservative government in Britain during the 1980s. The relevant acts of parliament give neither status nor protection to the employees, while the consumers' voice is hardly to be heard within the company's legal structure. To substitute a private for a public monopoly without adequately protecting either the employees or consumers is scarcely the way to create a society of responsible companies. Before a government nationalises or denationalises, the prior need is for the general acceptance of a philosophy of the company that satisfies the requirements of justice and participation.

4
The True Meaning of the Invisible Hand

The publication in 1776 of *The Wealth of Nations* by Adam Smith ushered in the modern science of economics. It is the classic plea for free trade, private enterprise and limited government. Smith wished to confine government to defence, justice and public services like education and transport. He strongly believed in the profit motive. When men are persuaded to invest money for profit, they are, said Smith, led by an invisible hand to promote an end – the public welfare – that was no part of their intention. To make the point clear, he added that he had never known much good done by those who affected to trade for the public good, while for any statesman to attempt to direct private people as to how they ought to employ their capital was folly and presumption.[1]

To understand Adam Smith's invisible hand we must return to the moral order of which he was writing and in which he believed. In a lecture in 1755, he had said 'little else is required to carry a state to the highest degree of opulence from the lowest barbarism but peace, easy taxes, and a tolerable administration of justice, all the rest being brought about by the natural order of things.' This reliance on 'natural order' anticipates Smith's discussion of it in 1759 in his first major work, *The Theory of Moral Sentiments*. There he uses the phrase 'the invisible hand' to describe the process by which wealth is automatically passed from the rich to the poor via consumption and investment: what Keynesians today would call the multiplier factor. By the time Smith wrote *The Wealth of Nations*, the invisible hand had become an automatic regulator of prosperity.

How are we to account for this optimism in the working of natural forces? The answer lies in the kind of society England and Scotland were when Smith was writing *The Wealth of Nations*.

It was written over a period of fifteen years from 1761 to 1776 – a time when the age of classicism and stability and of 'unchallenged assumptions' was drawing to an end. The industrial revolution had scarcely begun. Roads and canals were beginning to join the industrial towns of the Midlands to their markets, but it would be the end of the century before the factory system would supplant the traditional cottage and domestic method of production. Many of the inventions destined to change Britain from a rural to an industrial nation were conceived at this time, but James Watt's steam engine was not invented until 1769 and was not used in a cotton mill before 1785. Railways were still fifty years away, and cars would not be thought of for another century. In textiles, Hargreaves' spinning jenny (1767), Arkwright's water frame (1769) and Crompton's mule (1775) were among the most important inventions, but their application would take another generation to accomplish the transfer of the textile industry from home to factory. Domestic and small-scale production were still the rule.

Adam Smith's belief in natural forces, the open market and the invisible hand was not shared by John Ruskin who, in 1862, wrote that he knew no previous instance in human history of a nation's establishing a systematic disobedience to the first principles of its professed religion.[2] At first sight Smith and Ruskin appear poles apart in their thinking. But if we study with care the arguments each advances and the conditions in which each wrote, we shall find Smith not so far from Ruskin as is generally supposed. By training and inclination, Smith was a moral philosopher. In his philosophy he reflects the optimistic outlook of Frances Hutcheson, his friend and immediate predecessor in the chair of moral philosophy at the University of Glasgow. The key word in Hutcheson's moral philosophy is 'benevolence' – this being the quality required of human beings to enable them to associate for their own welfare and protection.

In his lectures on moral philosophy at the University of Glasgow, Smith took natural theology as his starting point, followed by its application to the individual (ethics), to society as a whole (jurisprudence), and finally to men at work (political economy). Behind all his lectures lay the concept of a natural law governing human existence. In the words of John Locke (1690): 'The Law of Nature stands as an Eternal Rule to all men, legislators as well as others. The rules that they make for other mens' actions must . . . be conformable to the Law of Nature, i.e. to the Will of God of which it is a declaration.'[3]

Thomas Hobbes approached the subject even more directly in *De Corpore Politico* (1650): 'The sum of Gods' law is "thou shalt love thy neighbour as thyself" and the same is the sum of the Law of Nature.'[4] To the natural law philosopher the golden rule of doing unto others as you would be done by is also the rule of human interdependence and mutuality. It accords with reason and revelation. The reasonable man acting reasonably is of the essence of British common law, while equity relies on conscience, the key to which Hobbes gives in his summary of the natural law: 'There is an easy rule to know upon a sudden, whether the action I be to do, be against the Law of Nature, or not. And it is but this: that a man imagine himself in the place of the Party with whom he hath to do, and reciprocally him in his.'[5]

A recent definition of natural law is that of the jurist Sir Frederick Pollock, who writes that it is 'an ultimate principle of fitness with regard to the nature of man as a rational and social animal,' and 'The sum of the principles founded in human nature which determine the conduct befitting him in his rational and social quality.'[6]

The fact that Adam Smith was a natural law philosopher is clear from many passages in his writings, of which two will serve to illustrate the rest:

> By acting . . . [morally] we necessarily pursue the most effectual means for promoting the happiness of mankind, and may therefore be said, in some sense, to co-operate with the Deity.
>
> All the members of human society stand in need of each other's assistance . . . where the necessary assistance is reciprocally afforded . . . the society flourishes and is happy.[7]

Thus, 'the invisible hand' of Adam Smith represents not so much the interplay of unrestrained impersonal economic forces, as the hand of Providence working through the family as a unit of social and local responsibility; a company of responsible individuals in a local society, in which the approbation of his fellow men restrained the entrepreneur by constantly reminding him of his duty as a parent and citizen.

The advent of large-scale industrialism, centralised finance and limited liability destroyed the delicate balance between 'benevolence' and the desire for economic advance, which had been taken for granted by Adam Smith and formed part of the natural law tradition. As a political economist, Smith sought to free the individual to pursue his own interest, believing that the resulting spin-off would benefit the poor more than any government action could do. As a moral and natural law philosopher, he assumed that the desire to be well thought of in the community and in the eyes of one's family and neighbours would be sufficient to preserve an underlying justice in social arrangements. This is not to pretend that Adam Smith's philosophy and economics are altogether reconcilable. There is a tension between them nowhere satisfactorily resolved, probably because he was not himself aware of it. Its existence has been discussed at length in connection with Adam Smith's bicentenary.[8] For us this tension in Smith's writing is valuable as a comment on our own dilemma. That dilemma is how, in the interests of justice, to control the great power structures which have arisen in industry and finance, without creating a universal state bureaucracy.

We have seen that Adam Smith believed in a natural order based on 'benevolence' or mutuality, which is the cardinal principle of the natural law. He was still thinking in terms of the unit of enterprise as a family or, if it were a company, a chartered company with clear social responsibilities. Were Smith alive today we should find him vigorously analysing the public company to see how it carries out its multiple reponsibilities. He would be in favour of the limitation of dividends. In *The Wealth of Nations* he advocates a maximum interest allowable by law of five per cent[9] (this was before the age of inflation), at a time when British government funds stood at three per cent a year. He would have demanded control over monopolies and price rings and would have been in favour of government intervention for this purpose. He would support the consumer movement and press for consumer organisations to be given their proper place alongside employers and trades unions in the discussion of national industrial policy. At the same time, he would have warned us against supposing that government can replace the private owner as an innovator and creator of fresh enterprise. It is certain Smith would have questioned the powers and rights of the monolithic power structures we have seen grow up in the past fifty years in private industry, the nationalised corporations and the trades unions.

What Adam Smith would have sought, and what we must seek, is to make these organisations conform to the law of human mutuality. Smith believed that social balance could be established by combining family responsibility with private enterprise. The invisible hand can be trusted only when it is at the service of a moral agent which, in Adam Smith's time, was the family. If we wish to follow him, we will seek a way of combining enterprise with responsibility in the modern public company and corporation. This is the way of the responsible company.

5
The Sources of Managerial Authority

What do we understand by authority and whence is it derived? Is it conferred by God, as Charles I thought, or by the consent of those it affects: the people? And if authority is conferred by those it affects, can it also be withdrawn by them? This is the position John Locke took in the controversy over authority in the Civil War. Thomas Hobbes held an opposing view. He demonstrated that authority once conferred becomes unconditional, because decisions have finally to be made by one person. Someone has to decide, if anarchy is to be avoided. Both philosophers used the Civil War to prove their case: Hobbes to justify the conduct of Charles I, Locke to defend the Parliamentarians. Subsequent history would seem to show that the truth lies somewhere between them. We may agree that authority is necessary, and in its exercise absolute, because it is indivisible in action. But when authority acts unreasonably or unconstitutionally, it is likely to be challenged and, if challenged successfully, lost. So it proved in the Civil War. And so it is with management in a company today.

Because business decisions have generally to be made against time, management needs to have prior authority in order to manage effectively. In the last war Winston Churchill is said to have told Professor Lindemann that he had chosen him to be the government's chief scientific adviser because he wanted a man who could make 'irrevocable decisions on insufficient evidence'. What is true in war is often true of business. The future is rarely foreseeable, while investment decisions about new products have to be made months and even years in advance. New energy resources may require a lead time of as much as ten years before production. All business involves risk-taking. Apart from the competitive uncertainties, there is a fluctuating economy and a constantly changing political power struggle to be taken into account, to say nothing of famine, flood and earthquake. All this makes it necessary for business management to have prior authority to act. Joint consultation may be desirable but may not be practicable in a competitive and uncertain world.

What gives a man or an idea authority? The meaning of the word 'authority' embraces authorship, as the word implies. The author is the imaginer; the person who embodies and represents an idea. It may be the idea of making a product, a story or a poem; whatever it is, the author is the instigator, creator, spokesman, champion, promoter and generator. Behind the words 'author' and 'authority' lies the idea of enlargement; the promise of a wider scope. The man of authority in a company is the manager. He represents an idea, in this case of a company.

There are different kinds of authority; inner and outer, original and derived. Inner authority in a person is the result of moral certainty. The man who has conviction has a natural authority, and leadership is often the result. Outer authority may be conferred by formal or legal process, such as the election of a prime minister by the members of his party, or of a board of directors by a company's shareholders.

Original authority is enjoyed by parents because of their responsibility for their children. The same is true of the proprietor of a business which he has himself created and for which he takes responsibility. Discipline (the corollary of authority) will be accepted where the risk of failure is perceived and shared. Nothing makes for social cohesion like a shared hazard. The family business in its first phase has the advantages of smallness. Its purpose is clear and communicates itself in a direct way which cannot easily be imitated in a company where large numbers are involved in a complex enterprise in which the individual worker plays only a very small part. In a large business, authority tends to be derived and delegated. It is derived from the shareholders in general meeting and delegated by them to the board of directors and by the board to the managing director and line management.

There is, however, another form of authority, an inherent or original authority coming up from the shop floor. This is the authority of the process itself. The shop-floor worker knows what has to be done and has often discovered, or will discover by trial and error, how best to do it. This knowledge represents the accumulated wisdom of shop-floor experience and it is part of the task of the foreman to see that it is communicated upwards to management. Thus authority in business is another name for the willingness and capacity of individuals to submit to the necessities of co-operative systems. It is 'the process by which the individual delegates to the organisation responsibility for an organisational decision.'[1]

The most efficient form of management will be that which engages the consent and co-operation of the workforce by aligning formal authority with the inner authority that comes from the job and the people who work on the shop floor. This fusion of authority becomes all the more necessary as business grows bigger in scale and more complex. There is a large reserve of productivity latent in human attitudes on the shop floor. It is the single biggest resource we have. If we could tap that resource, the growth of productivity would be explosive. Nothing holds us back from increased production but ourselves. It is not a question of redesigning our factories or of huge investment in new plant. Before we deploy scarce capital resources we need to maximise productivity using the resources we already have. No expert known to the writer who has quantified the reservoir of productivity latent in shop-floor attitudes in Britain has put the potential increase below thirty per cent. Some have given a much higher figure. In the three-day working week during the strike of 1974, production remained practically normal in British industry.

The need for management to have real as distinct from formal or outward authority is seen in the lamentable story of two British concerns in 1980. In the case of *The Times*, a great newspaper was put out of action for eleven months by the inability of its directors to achieve management by consent. In face of the challenge of the trades unions, the authority of *The Times'* management broke down. That failure cost its proprietor seventy million pounds and achieved nothing. The 1980 strike of the steel unions against the British Steel Corporation was no less unfortunate. A three-month strike resulted in the loss of a quarter of British Steel's regular customers, some irretrievably. In both cases the authority of management disappeared when tested, with unhappy results for employees and the community. No one gained from these outbreaks of industrial madness, which demonstrate the compelling force of a collective purpose and its power to overcome individual rational judgement. The 1985 coal strike again showed the lengths to which men will go when driven by a collective will, and the high price that may have to be paid for the recovery of managerial authority once it is lost.

The peculiar power of a collective will resides in its limitation. The ordinary worker has a wide variety of purposes – personal, social, sporting, artistic or political. By comparison the trade union to which he belongs has only a limited purpose. Its very limitation enables its purpose to be held with a force which compels compliance even at the expense of the individual's judgement and interests, so it is not possible to overcome a collective will by offering individual incentives. The only solution is to create a collective will in the company stronger than the collective will of the unions, and there is but one way this can be done. It has to be done by creating a form of company which will attract a loyalty greater than the union can command. That means converting the company into a genuine fellowship based on an appropriate legal structure, in the same way that the wider national community accepts the rule of law as the basis of corporate life.

We can now see why the purpose of the company has to be changed *before* there can be a change in the workers' collective attitude to the company. Individually, the worker may trust management and feel a strong sense of loyalty to his work. But collectively he is bound to strike when told because the union represents the security which resides in the collective will. What is needed for management to recover its authority is a fresh sense of purpose that offers the individual worker a greater security than can his union. It must be a purpose shared between management and the workers in a company, and therefore a common purpose. But before there can be a common purpose there must first be a purpose, and this involves three things: an act of intellect, an act of will, and its communication, as Sir Oliver (later Lord) Franks explained to an audience at the London School of Economics when relating his wartime experiences at the Ministry of Supply:

> Unity of purpose was the essential presupposition of successful organisation . . . If any organisation is to have unity of purpose, it is obvious that there must be a purpose. It is obvious too that this purpose must be understood and accepted by the members of the organisation so that they are unified by it. What is a purpose? It is an idea, the product of the intellect; but it is also an idea affirmed by the will so that it becomes an objective of action. If it is to be the purpose of the members of the

organisation, it must be communicated and commended to them so that it is accepted as a common objective of their joint action. Without the act of intellect, the act of will and the act of communication, unity of purpose cannot be achieved.[2]

In its relations with the workforce the ultimate source of management's authority must be its concern for justice. This means holding to a purpose that seeks to balance the interests of those it serves. Holding a just balance in human affairs is no light task. It means working to principle rather than expediency, taking long views which may require times of waiting and recuperation from adverse market forces. To be successful in its balancing role, management needs all the help it can get, including the backing of a company law which supports its search for an acceptable corporate purpose.

6
The Challenge of Social Responsibility

Ultimate control of the policy of public limited companies still rests in the hands of shareholders because they alone have the legal power to dismiss the directors. In practice the control has been passing elsewhere, as the return on equity capital in the UK reveals. As we have seen (on page 21) the real net return to British equity shareholders over the period 1948–74 was 2.6 per cent per annum after tax, apart from capital gains. This is hardly sufficient incentive for the individual saver and it is not surprising that he increasingly prefers putting his money into private property he can enjoy, like houses, pictures and furniture, or spending it on holidays before it loses value by inflation. This option is not available to pension funds and insurance companies, which are bound to protect their clients' savings to the best of their ability by investments which show a cash return, such as land, buildings and equity shares. As a result, private holdings of shares in public companies are declining (other than in the case of some privatised companies, where special offers have been made), while the amount held by the institutions is increasing. If this trend continues, and there is every sign of its doing so, the basis of capitalism as we have known it – the private investor – will have disappeared before the end of the century.

The more ably-managed companies (including giants like Shell, BP and ICI) have sought to come to terms with the problem of diminishing shareholder support by encouraging the shareholders to take an interest in the company while, at the same time, moving towards an understanding with the workforce about the company's objectives. The identification of the company's social responsibilities is part of this chain of policy, which includes writing codes of conduct as a way of strengthening the authority of management, as we shall see in Chapter 7.

No doubt one reason for the awakening of interest in the large company to the question of its social responsibilities is the wish to anticipate, and if possible to discourage, state interference. But this is unlikely to be the sole motive. Industrial psychologists, ever since the work of Elton Mayo[1] in the 1930s, have been telling us that the attitude of the employees to the company is crucial to its success. To attempt to codify a company's social responsibilities is a way of engaging employees in a search for a common purpose, and the experience of Shell UK[2] is that it can bring about a marked attitude change for the better. But it raises difficult problems for management. How far should a company go in accepting social responsibilities? Since it cannot take the place of the state or do the work of a local authority, should it attempt to interfere at all in the affairs of the locality? Should the company not confine itself to making the best possible product at the lowest possible price?

Among academics, Professor Milton Friedman in the USA and Professor Hayek in Austria have spoken for those who think that firms should have as little to do with social responsibility as possible. Their argument is that it is for the state to legislate to compel companies to obey minimum standards in regard to such matters as land use, pollution of the atmosphere and noise. But legislation generally follows, rather than precedes, the abuse. Steel producers are an example of this. Throughout the 1950s Stewarts & Lloyds were digging up the countryside of Northamptonshire in search of iron ore for their Corby steel works. It was some years before the government passed legislation imposing on companies the legal duty of reinstating fields and woods devastated by open-cast mining, and by then it was too late to recover much of the amenity value lost. Unless companies can be persuaded to carry out their social responsibilities voluntarily, a socialist government will always be tempted to nationalise the company, and this is what eventually happened to Stewarts & Lloyds. Today that company has ceased to exist as a separate entity and the Corby steel works is closed. But nationalisation does not eliminate the problem; it merely removes it to another level. Instead of relying on *ad hoc* legislation, we need to build into the structure of the large company a concern for the interests of the surrounding community which will ensure that it takes continuous account of its responsibilities before, not after, damaging the environment. This means that management must be free to develop a holistic attitude towards its role.

What is holism? *The Concise Oxford Dictionary* says it is the 'tendency in nature to form wholes that are more than the sum of the parts by creative evolution.' The invention of the word 'holism' is attributed to General Smuts. In *Holism and Evolution* he writes:

> The creation of wholes, and ever more highly organised wholes, is an inherent character of the Universe . . . the whole-making tendency is seen at all stages of existence . . . with its roots in the inorganic, this universal tendency attains clear expression in the organic biological world, and reaches its highest expressions and results on the mental and spiritual planes of existence . . . wholes of various grades are the real units of Nature. Wholeness is the most characteristic expression of the nature of the universe in its forward movement in time.[3]

One observes the limited liability company following this evolutionary pattern of becoming a whole of a new kind, in which the acquisitive instinct is increasingly modified to conform with social need and purpose. As will be explained in Chapter 14, nationalisation is a short cut aimed at achieving this end. If it has failed, it is because organic growth cannot be forced in this way. It must be induced, and the law's role should be to assist that process, not to force it.

Many businessmen distrust the evolution of the company into wholeness. 'Where will it end?' they ask. 'How is one to equate economic necessity with social betterment within a company and retain efficiency and adequate control?' Once a company accepts its 'social responsibilities', whatever that is taken to mean, has it not written a blank cheque and handed it to others?

At first glance the horizon of social responsibility appears to be almost without limit. So is it natural that businessmen should fear its acceptance as a duty. But the fear is irrational, because it overlooks the control which the company exercises in its relationships with the community. In this respect the position of a company is not unlike that of a man or woman. Individuals develop their personality through social relationships. In the same way, a company's personality, and with it the loyalty and involvement of its workforce, develops through its social relationships. Like the individual, the capacity of the company to respond to any particular challenge is limited. But the holistic outlook is the healthy one as the word implies; both 'healthy' and 'whole' being derived from the early English word *hal* which is also the root of the word 'holy'.

Managers of businesses, large and small, will not fear the holistic outlook once they grasp the fact that in personal life they face it at every moment. Under God, each of us has to meet a constant stream of claims upon our time, energy and money – from wife or husband, home, children, institutions and charities, friends, neighbourhood, country and church. Social life involves continuous choice, and we can only partly do justice to the manifold claims made upon us, since our understandings as well as our means are limited and only partly tell us how we should respond. What matters is that we should be constantly aware of the claims of others upon us and be willing to respond within our limited capacities, means and time.

The same is true of a company. It, too, has to deal with a constant series of claims upon it, not only from its customers, employees and shareholders, but from the community of which it is a member. Holism means accepting the situation and doing one's best in the circumstances, not running away from reality but taking all aspects of reality into account in making corporate decisions. This requires a certain managerial philosophy and a corresponding style of management. Instead of regarding the profit-and-loss figure as the only criterion of success, it means a finely-tuned and balanced response to competing claims. In a sentence, it means a company's pursuing justice and balance rather than maximum short-term gain. In the big company this is already happening, if not from choice, through increasing social pressures on those who direct and manage public companies.

When in personal life we fall ill and the illness is serious, we take to our beds until the doctor tells us to get up. If an operation becomes necessary, we go into hospital. In both cases we are obliged to drop our normal activities for a time. We do this not from choice but from necessity.

The same is true of a company. If it makes a loss and is unable to satisfy the claims of its employees and shareholders, the company may have to curtail for a time its social activities and its social responses. The less the state in the meantime has had to legislate to enforce social responsibility, the freer the individual company will be to recover its health quickly – an additional reason for the voluntary acceptance of social responsibility rather than waiting until it is imposed by legislation.

There is nothing for a company to fear in accepting and defining its social responsibilities, and much to be gained, particularly when it involves the workforce in choosing corporate goals and accepting corporate restraints. The holistic view of the company also provides an answer to inflation – perhaps the only sure answer – for it creates a common interest with labour that looks to tomorrow rather than today. Inflation is both a sign and a consequence of a lack of faith in the future. Because the holistic outlook requires the balancing of claims, it necessarily takes the long view, for the future is part of the equation. Only when the workers realise that they in a sense belong to the company and the company represents their future, does it become possible for them to take the long view. Even then management will, by moral consistency, have to convince the workforce of its devotion to the holistic view. Moral consistency of this kind does not exclude self-interest, since the company's first duty is to be healthy and increase its resources in such a way as to satisfy its shareholders, customers and workers. Moral consistency also demands taking a positive attitude to the company's social responsibilities. Managements have been known to damage their image through neglect of this truism. Workers are quick to size up the true aims of management, and a single incident may reveal what they are. A shop steward in an engineering works was heard to approach his supervisor and say: 'Bert hasn't been in for two weeks. He lives alone and may be ill. Can we send someone along to see if everything is OK?' to which the reply was: 'It's nothing to do with us, go and tell the union official.'

Within a company, management must exercise its authority, or cease to manage. But in its relations with the community, and particularly with the immediate neighbourhood, management has to learn to take a subordinate role. This is particularly true of housing and amenities such as sports grounds and play areas where there is a risk that the company may otherwise divide the community. In Middlewich, Cheshire, in the 1950s, ICI bought expensive instruments for their local brass band and the town brass could not compete. To split the community in this way caused jealousy and was a mistake. To do ICI justice, the mistake was recognised and put right.

On the whole employees do not want to be treated as 'company men'. They want to be free. One way in which a company can serve the local community without seeking to organise its employees outside the office or plant is by encouraging them to stand for local elections or in other ways to serve their local communities. In Germany, The Karl Zeiss Stiftung of Jena, as long ago as 1896, provided in its articles of trust that any of its employees elected to official positions in the community would automatically be given the necessary leave of absence and be paid their normal fixed time wage while doing so. Sears Roebuck in Chicago has for many years encouraged its employees to play an active role in the communities where the company has plant and offers to finance community projects in which its employees take an active interest.

When a company decides to set aside a proportion of its profits for the purpose of assisting the locality, it may be desirable to consult its employees rather than for the directors to hand out donations under pressure from the directors of other companies on the basis of 'you support us and we will support you'. When in 1957 the Economist Intelligence Unit surveyed the donations of British public companies, it found that the average amount per company was somewhat less than one per cent of gross profits. A similar inquiry in 1985 revealed that the average of 1,000 of the largest British companies had dropped to one-third of one per cent of gross profits.

Where a money gift is the main measure of corporate social involvement there is the danger that the contribution to the community will be regarded as self-interested and peripheral. Society looks to the company above all to provide jobs. When bad times come, the company may find itself obliged to lay off or discharge employees. The company's attitude at this point goes to the root of its social responsibility, all the more so when the micro-processor and computer are threatening to replace labour in the factory on an unprecedented scale. Several British firms, including Pilkingtons, ICI and the British Steel Corporation, have in these circumstances, and under union pressure, lent their active assistance and resources to finding alternative employment for workers they have had to discharge. This practice may still be unusual in Britain, but it appears to have become standard practice in Japan, where some of the larger firms and their employees are linked by a system of reciprocal obligation which is lifelong. When a Japanese business takes a school-leaver into its employ it usually accepts responsibility for him for the rest of his working life. This is known in Japan as the 'lifetime employment' system.[4]

There is mutual advantage to be gained from providing the worker with as much security as possible. Japanese employers find it encourages their managers to develop a growth psychology and leads to the conception of new products and services.

Loyalty breeds loyalty and trust inspires trust. We need in British industry to find a similar virtuous cycle to replace the vicious spiral of acrimony and resistance to change based on fear.

How does a company mark out its own special area of social responsibility without undertaking more than it can manage or neglecting its primary economic role? In an individual, the problem of meeting conflicting external claims is resolved by an inner direction, which in more religiously inclined days was known as a sense of vocation. We still talk of a person following his calling; and 'calling' implies challenge and response. A company is like an individual in this respect. It, too, will develop a bias or vocation towards a certain type of social involvement, and a wise state will encourage firms to develop a variety of responses. The company I represented in the UK for forty years – International Paper – is one of the largest landowners in North America. The company owns or has cutting rights over several million acres of forest, with its rivers, lakes, fish and game. In the forests the company's policy is one of permanent replacement, while at the same time encouraging their use for recreation by the public in such a way as to avoid forest fires and to protect the balance of nature. If International Paper over the years has earned a reputation for being a good employer and neighbour, it is as much through its social as its employment policies. These two aspects of industrial relations are interdependent. Bad relations within a community will spill over into the factory. Bad relations in the factory can sour a community.

The special problem of a company in the position of being a sole employer is paternalism. However good the company and however broad its objectives, men and women desire to be free. In a town dominated by one employer the truest expression of social concern may be to encourage others to take responsibility in the community and for the employer to fade into the background. There is no simple formula by which we can say in advance what area of social responsibility a company should accept. It all depends on the circumstances. In a time of falling employment the first priority may be to help people to employ themselves. This attitude was well expressed by the chairman of Shell when, in the course of a lecture in 1977, he said: 'I believe that big companies should establish a positive management policy which recognises the value of the small enterprise ... and resolve to support this in action.'[5]

To help the smaller company establish itself as a supplier of services or parts to the large public company, or to seek ways of developing new businesses and encouraging company employees to start businesses of their own, has not hitherto been regarded as a responsibility of the large enterprise. But Shell and a number of other companies have accepted this task in the spirit of wholeness which it has been the purpose of this chapter to describe.

7
Finding an Agreed Objective

Between the two world wars unemployment in Britain only once fell below ten per cent. That was in 1927. The average unemployment rate between 1921 and 1938 was over fourteen per cent of the insured population.[1] Under these conditions, discipline in industry was maintained by fear of the sack and unemployment. The introduction of the welfare state after 1943 largely removed these fears and with them the discipline fear had previously imposed on the workforce. In the 1950s and 1960s British unemployment averaged less than Beveridge's minimum of three per cent. Furthermore, its effect was cushioned by the benefits offered by the welfare state, which included unemployment pay, sickness benefits, and supplementary allowances which even covered the families of men on strike. Thus protected, the workers for the first time in modern history could look their employers in the face without fear.

Meantime, continuity of production and supply had grown ever more essential to maintain the life of an advanced industrialised society. As a result the workers in key industries like the mines, docks, electricity supply and newspapers could through the organisation of the closed shop enforce their own conditions of work and, to a large extent, its remuneration. Sir William (afterwards Lord) Beveridge's book *Full Employment in a Free Society* had come out in 1944. This book, together with Maynard (afterwards Lord) Keynes's *General Theory of Employment, Interest and Money* (1936), set the stage for the introduction of the welfare state in Britain after the Second World War.

One day, meeting Sir William Beveridge at the Reform Club, I asked him what he thought would have to be done if the workers, under full employment, were to decide to take full advantage of their strength. He thought for a moment and replied, 'In that case we should have to nationalise industry.' I thought this reply inadequate, and doubted if Sir William had thought the problem out. The only discussion of it comes near the end of his book, where he notes that the first objective must be to get us around the next corner – mass unemployment and the fear of unemployment – and he adds: 'The problems that lie beyond that corner will become clearer when that corner has been passed; they can, if we so desire, be left to be dealt with when they are reached.'[2]

Lord Keynes also left the question of industrial discipline under full employment in a state of uncertainty. When questioned by a correspondent he replied, 'I do not doubt that a serious problem will arise as to how wages are to be restrained when we have a combination of collective bargaining and full employment,' but he went no further and offered no solution.

It seemed to me then, as it does now, that without greater commitment to the purposes of the company, organised labour could not be expected to forego the use of its own power for the sake of the future. If this were true, we might need to create a new kind of company, in which the worker would face the need for restraint in his own interest and not merely because someone told him it was necessary to avoid inflation. In 1951 I wrote:

> Industry in the twentieth century can no longer be regarded as a private arrangement for enriching shareholders. It has become a joint enterprise in which workers, management, consumers, the locality, government and trade union officials all play a part. If the system which we know by the name of private enterprise is to continue, some way must be found to embrace the many interests which go to make up industry in a common purpose. The tension between the parties to industry, such as that between the workers and shareholders, is at present being resolved by hit-or-miss methods: by strike, negotiation, and compromise, leading to a further process in the same order, and so on *ad infinitum*. The alternative is to create a structure in industry which recognises each of the parties as having certain definite rights, and provides for those rights (with their corresponding responsibilities) in the legal constitution of the single company, in such a way that the tension in industry may become capable of resolution at the board-room table of the individual enterprise. But before this is possible there must first be discovered in industry a basis of justice upon which to raise the structure of co-operation. It must take account of all the parties involved in the actual conduct of industry. Since it is the legal structure of the company which determines its formal responsibilities to the parties to industry, we must

examine the legal structure of the limited liability company and see to what extent it is capable of adaptation, to make possible full co-operation between the parties to industry on a basis of justice. From this study it may be discovered what are the changes needed in the practice of companies to make them socially responsible, and the alterations required in the law of companies to make the acceptance of social responsibility by industry possible . . . The danger is that sooner or later the strains imposed on central government by an out-of-date legal structure in industry will prove too great for the continuance of democracy.[3]

It has taken a generation for British management to take up the challenge of clarifying the social responsibility of business as a means of working towards a better understanding with the labour force. It was not until 1973 that the Company Affairs Committee of the Confederation of British Industry (CBI) recommended that in any fresh company legislation, companies should be encouraged

to recognise duties and obligations (within the context of the objects for which the company was established) arising from the company's relationships with creditors, suppliers, customers, employees and society at large; and in so doing to exercise their best judgment to strike a balance between the interests of the aforementioned groups and between the interests of those groups and the interests of the proprietors of the company.[4]

The lead having been given, the British Institute of Management followed in 1976 by urging on their members the acceptance of a code of corporate behaviour, together with a statement of a company's social responsibilities. The BIM published a summary of steps already taken in this direction by a number of well-known firms, including Turner & Newall, CIBA-Geigy UK, and Rio Tinto-Zinc.[5]

Such a code of conduct can go some way towards educating management in the complex nature of its responsibilities and the manner of reconciling them. But, being voluntary and liable to change, it cannot satisfy labour, particularly organised labour, that it marks a watershed in industrial policy which will protect the worker against the loss of his job, or unfair discrimination. Since 1971 the British worker has been protected by law against unfair dismissal, after a qualifying period, but this does not give him any status within the company. He may be an employee but he is still a stranger to the company, not being regarded as a member of the corporate body unless he chooses to buy one or more of the company's shares in the market.

If the workers in British industry and commerce are to be asked to exercise moderation in the pursuit of higher wages, restraining present demands in the interest of future growth and corporate strength, something more radical is required to overcome the historic conflict between the agents of capital and labour. What is required, and what alone can break the impasse, is a determination on both sides to seek justice rather than maximum short-term gain and to do so through the company and its organs. Since it is the company which suffers from distrust, it is in the company that the remedy for distrust must be found. What is needed is to find a purpose capable of binding men together in a joint enterprise.

It is obvious, as Lord Franks said in the lecture quoted on page 32, that if an organisation is to have unity of purpose, it must first have a purpose. Moreover, it must be a purpose understood and accepted by the members of the organisation. But companies are not required by the law to state what their purpose is. All that company law in Britain requires is that the memorandum of association – the foundation document of the company – contain a clause describing its objectives in general terms. Thus a company may state its objectives as being to print and publish a newspaper and do all such acts as are ancillary to printing and publishing. But it need not describe the kind of newspaper it intends to publish or the principles, such as truth, independence and editorial freedom, it intends to pursue.

All these are omitted from the memorandum of association which is concerned with means and not with ends. But corporate loyalty depends on agreement about ends even more than about means. Unless the employees of a company know what the real purpose of the company is and their role in it, how can they be expected to give the company their loyalty and confidence? In the example given, the newspaper may be a subsidiary of a foreign corporation which in turn may be controlled by a foreign and potentially hostile power. There may be no intention to promote a permanent business; the true purpose may be to influence public opinion for a limited time and for a particular purpose. None of this need be disclosed in the existing memorandum of association.

Company law assumes that shareholders, and they alone, are 'members' of the company, and since shareholders as a class generally look to their dividends as the object of their investment, the real purpose of a company is seen to be maximum profit for the shareholders' benefit. If this is true, it is not one calculated to inspire the workforce. Management is aware of a conflict of purpose and knows as a practical reality that in a company, especially in a large organisation, an economic and a social system exist side by side, both of which require to be satisfied if there is to be efficiency.

It was this realisation that led Shell UK to launch its UK Development Programme in 1965. There had been a succession of disputes in the UK refineries and restrictive practices were widespread. Management's relations with shop stewards and unions were marked by 'deep distrust and suspicion', and productivity was low. At this point the management of Shell set up an employee relations planning group to consider what needed to be done to improve industrial relations and, with it, productivity.[6] Paul Hill, in a brilliant analysis of the successful experiment, said the men were fundamentally not committed to the company's objective, perhaps because that objective had never been defined. The investigating team set out to induce employees' commitment to company objectives without which only a small part of workers' potential was being utilised. Assisted by the Tavistock Institute of Human Relations, the team defined the purpose of Shell and submitted this statement of purpose to the workforce and management for review, criticism and adoption.

The resulting agreed formulation of company objectives converted the stock answer of 'maximisation of long-term profitability' into the optimisation of all the resources involved in the business, including men, equipment and the environment. Shell does not regard itself as owning these resources, but as holding them in trust to make the best possible use of them on behalf of the community. Management is thus seen to be in a position of trust, pledged to do its best simultaneously to develop people and to pay regard to community needs, while at the same time striving to maximise productivity. A balance has to be struck which involves the reconciliation of what in the short run may seem contradictory aims – economic efficiency and human welfare – but in the long run can be shown to be complementary. In the words of the book's epilogue (by Eric Trist of the Tavistock Institute):

> Any valid and acceptable philosophy . . . would have to postulate the existence of a social as well as an economic object for the company.

> This meant reconciling the one with the other. Satisfactory criteria for doing this had never been established.
>
> A first step . . . was found by working out the implications of a basic duality: that the assets of the company were at the same time the resources of society. The assets it 'owned', most especially its human assets, were not owned absolutely but conditionally. The conditions of the company's being allowed to continue to use them were that these resources would not be exploited or degraded but protected and developed. (p. 197)

> In short, the economic objective supplies the necessary condition but the social objective the sufficient condition for the survival and growth of the enterprise. The fundamental fallacy is to suppose that the necessary and sufficient conditions both lie in the economic objective; yet this has been the traditional assumption. The social objective is not simply a constraint on the economic objective; one is the co-producer of the other. (p. 198)

The resulting declaration of purpose was accepted both by management and by the employees of Shell UK and endorsed by the unions, in the case of the Transport & General Workers Union shop stewards with enthusiasm. The company's declared intention to develop people's potentialities to the full and rationalise terms and conditions of employment, treating management and workers alike as regards methods of payment, facilities and concessions, was especially welcomed. This experiment, in seeking to establish a common purpose in a business enterprise, is a model of what needs to be done on a national scale.

PART 2
A SOLUTION

8 The General Purposes Clause

If he is to give the company his emotional assent and the benefit of the doubt when his long-term interest differs from his immediate self-interest, the worker must know that corporate policy is trustworthy. This means setting some standard against which day-to-day policy decisions can be viewed. This was the method adopted by Shell. The investigating team of psychologists and anthropologists, the former questioning and the latter observing social behaviour, concluded that motivation was low because the workers did not feel committed to the corporate objectives, of which they were in any case ignorant. This meant that only a small part of the workers' potential could be realised. It also meant that management could not take risks involving the workers without prior consultation. They lacked a mandate to manage; such a mandate is essential in a competitive business where, as Lord Beaverbrook once observed to me, 'if you can be right more than fifty per cent of the time you are a genius.'

The statement of objectives eventually adopted by Shell – and printed with its 1979 Annual Report – reads:

> Shell companies recognise inter-related responsibilities in business to shareholders to protect and provide a return on their investment; to customers for quality, price and service; to employees in recognition of their contribution; and to society for the conduct of the business in accord with good citizenship and proper regard to safety and the environment.

The logical place for such a declaration of a company's purpose is in its memorandum of association. This at present need specify only in general terms the business the company proposes to carry on, together with the powers needed for that purpose. Unfortunately, businessmen have brought into the memorandum every other power they can conceive of as required, to avoid the risk of being subsequently held to be *ultra vires*. The result has been to nullify the value of the rule.[1]

What is needed, as the CBI statement on the responsibilities of the public company makes clear, is an objects or general purposes clause in the memorandum which empowers the directors, within their chosen field of activity, to take into consideration the interests of the employees as well as the shareholders and the company's responsibilities to outside interests, including its customers and the locality. This means a general purposes clause giving directors of public companies the right and the duty of balancing to the best of their abilities the conflicting claims made upon them. This is to be done in the interests of the business itself and on the basis of seeking to give each constituent element what belongs to it. One cannot expect a general purposes clause in a new companies act to provide by itself a sufficient moral imperative, (see p. 45). What it can do is to give the directors of public companies support in seeking to create the optimum balance between the parties concerned – shareholders, employees, consumers and the community.

Since human nature desires to feel secure, it is important that the workers should have confidence in the company and its policies. The willingness of a company to express its objectives in human as well as in technical and financial terms, not as a one-off statement but as a pledge for the future, is a sign to the workforce that fairness is intended as a permanent ingredient of corporate policy and not just the brainchild of a particular individual. It makes a difference if the employees and their trades unions are able to see that the primary object of the company is to satisfy consumer need, and therefore that quality, price and reliability are legitimate goals of corporate policy and worthwhile objectives for a workforce seeking excellence and high reward.

The largest British company is British Petroleum. Like Shell UK, it made public in 1980 a statement of its corporate objectives:

> The BP Group's general objective is to conduct its business efficiently and profitably as an independent commercial concern, whilst carrying on its responsibilities in society, and thus to contribute to the wealth of the communities in which it operates. Its activities and operations should earn the approval of those communities, provide a service to customers which takes account of increasingly exacting requirements, and attract the willing co-operation of employees throughout the world. The measure of its success will be the increase in value of the business,

the shareholders' equity and the dividend, through profitable growth and maximum return on investment commensurate with risk.

Public companies in the USA have made similar declarations, sometimes on an industry-wide basis. American health and life insurance companies possess a 'Clearing House on Corporate Social Responsibility' to which over two hundred companies, representing eighty-five per cent of the industry, make regular returns of the projects they support or sponsor. These include youth activities, local health campaigns, neighbourhood improvement schemes and anti-pollution and safety programmes, involving part-time work, during office hours, for six thousand employees of the companies concerned and the expenditure of a billion dollars a year.

The cynic will attribute these developments to the desire to head off the unwanted attentions of government. It is true that the socially responsible company provides an alternative to nationalisation, and in this context the British Institute of Management has gone on record as saying that future company legislation should incorporate the concept of a company charter 'which would be granted to those companies whose codes are publicly acceptable and would give them a special standing.'[2]

Codes of conduct should not, however, be confused with corporate declarations of social responsibility. A code of conduct is a statement about business ethics as it concerns the company's personnel. It deals with matters like the taking of bribes and the misuse of inside information. It sets a standard for the behaviour expected of a company's executives. Its values lie in making people in a company think seriously about their behaviour and in confirming their authority in dealing with others, including employees, consumers and the government.

A company statement on social responsibility, like that of the oil company quoted, is a statement about corporate rather than individual objectives. It appeals to the principle of balance, and is a way of invoking justice. It recognises that the directors of public companies have multiple responsibilities. Since 1862 company law has required the directors of a company only to have regard to the shareholders' interests. But clause 46 of the 1980 Companies Act (repeated in section 309 of the consolidating Act of 1985) extends the matters to which the directors of a company shall have regard to 'the interests of the employees in general', and a footnote to the clause says that directors 'will need to balance the interests of the various classes of members.'

The immediate cause of this extension of directors' legal obligations was to overcome the difficulties in which the directors of the *Daily News* found themselves when they were taken to court for authorising a payment to the staff upon a winding-up. (*Parkes vs Daily News Ltd* 1962).

But section 309 as it now stands in the 1985 Companies Act would seem capable of a wider interpretation. What are the interests of the employees 'in general'? Are they confined to wages and benefits or would an unwanted takeover bid be relevant to their interests? What about consultation and information? Do these form a valid 'interest' of the employees to which the directors should have regard? In the Shell and BP statements we are seeing a recognition by two very large companies that their real purposes are manifold and cannot be constrained by the straitjacket of shareholder power.

We are moving into a new dimension in company law, that of trust; and it is trust, in a different sense, that has been the missing ingredient in industrial relations. Trust depends on mutuality, as we saw in Chapter 4, and mutuality is the essence of social morality, without which freedom is at risk. As Fred Hirsch has put it: 'The radical need is to accept that we may be near the limit of explicit social organisation possible without a social morality.'[3]

In the light of what has been said above let us now attempt to draft a suitable general purposes clause. Since everything depends on the company's health, its primary object must be its own survival and growth. So the first clause should read:

> To make the company economically and financially strong in order to ensure its continued growth and future development as a means of providing good service, secure employment and a fair return to its investors and shareholders.

Having established the company's survival and growth as the primary object, we must put into words the responsibility of the company to provide goods and services of the highest possible quality and at the lowest price consistent with the company's other objectives. It is excellence that must be the aim here.

Some would query this order of priority on the ground that the most important objective, once the survival of the company is assured, should be the interest of its employees. But in the long run, well-paid and secure employment can only be guaranteed by satisfied customers. Even where there is a monopoly, as in the nationalised coal industry or in the nationalised railway system, countervailing competition will in the end establish a decisive limit to the exploitation by labour of its monopoly power. The strong advocacy of nuclear power at Sizewell by the Central Electricity Generating Board is at least partly attributable to fear that the coal miners will continue to overplay their hand, and that this requires an alternative supply of energy, not subject to control by the National Union of Mineworkers.

It is wrong to put the worker before the consumer, for production exists for the sake of consumption, and not vice versa. We work for others, not for ourselves only, and in doing so we acknowledge our interdependence. In the words of William Temple:

> the reason why goods are produced is that men may satisfy their needs by consuming those goods. Production by its own natural law exists for consumption. If, then, a system comes into being in which production is regulated more by the profit obtainable for the producer than by the need of the consumer, that system is defying the Natural Law or Natural Order . . .[4]

In plainer and less exalted terms a team of American investigators into the causes of excellence in successful USA businesses concluded that putting the customers first was decisive, 'whether bending tin, frying hamburgers, or providing rooms for rent, virtually all of the excellent companies had, it seemed, defined themselves as *de facto* service businesses. Customers reign supreme.'[5]

The interest of the company's employees comes next in order of priority. The company's duty is to provide them with the best possible conditions of employment consistent with its other objectives, to give to all its employees the right of representation at any and every level they desire, and to encourage their personal development, promotion, and growth in skill, together with such security in work as is consistent with the company's growth and general objectives.

The individual worker should have a secure place in the objectives of the company. Since (as we saw in Chapter 3) the company is not just shareholders' property, but a living and growing organism with its own corporate personality, the workforce ought individually to be regarded as members of the company in natural law. The shareholders have, as a result of the passage of time and the development of the organisation into a public company, become creditors with certain definite rights, which do not, however, constitute ownership of the company in the eyes of the law, as we saw in Chapter 3 (see page 18).

The fact that a company is in reality people at work in the service of other people, does not conflict with management's obligation to the shareholders. But it limits that obligation to what is legitimate. When a company is losing money and is unable to pay a fair return on the shareholders' investment, which has been the case with much of the quoted company sector in Britain since the last war (see page 21), then shareholders' powers may need to be strengthened rather than weakened. In the nationalised industries the shareholder – namely the government – should either exercise its authority to resist a level of wages that forces the company into losses borne by the taxpayer (unless it is clearly the will of the electorate that a particular nationalised industry or company shall be supported on social grounds out of taxation), or privatise. The general rule should be self-dependence, and exceptions to this rule should be argued and accepted only on grounds of public policy.

The final section of the general purposes clause deals with the company's relations with government, local authorities and the local environment. Excellent formulations of this aspect of their social responsibility have been made by some of the companies which contributed to the BIM Survey of 1976.[6] A simple way to define the public company's social responsibility is to say that it shall be required to act towards the community in at least as responsible a manner as would be expected from a responsible individual citizen in similar circumstances.

The resulting general purposes clause – for comparison with the statements of Shell and BP quoted above – would read:

> To make the company economically and financially strong in order to ensure its continued growth and future development as a means of providing good service, secure employment and a fair return to its investors and shareholders.
>
> To provide goods and services of the best quality and the most reasonable prices consistent with its other objectives.
>
> To give its employees every reasonable opportunity for their interests to be heard within the company and for their promotion and development in skill and to allow reasonable time off for attention to public duties.
>
> To act towards the community of which it is a member in as responsible a manner as would be expected from a responsible citizen in like circumstances.

These are the necessary ingredients, if not the invariable mix, of a clause setting out the purposes of the company in general terms. A number of consequences will flow from its adoption. The company will have made a public declaration by which it will from time to time ask to be judged, whether by the public, by the consumer interests involved or by the trades unions acting on behalf of its members. This may well require an extension of the annual general meeting, as we shall see in Chapter 12. It may require the appointment of a referee or ombudsman to receive complaints and assist in interpreting the company's declared purpose (this will be discussed in Chapter 10). Finally, it will involve reconsideration of the company's relations with its shareholders over time. The next chapter deals with this.

9

*The Redemption of Equity Capital**

When a company is regarded as a social enterprise with multiple responsibilities and its directors' duties include the balancing of claims, we have arrived at a point where the question of the limits of reward to any one party must be faced.

There is philosophical and religious ground for thinking that the modern equity share is usurious. 'Usury' in the Middle Ages meant any bargain that was unjust, as R.H. Tawney has shown.[1] On this reading it is possible for a trade union to be guilty of usury if it seeks disproportionate advantage for its members at the expense of the company. But generally speaking, usury is the word used when considering the just reward of capital.

The shareholders who invested in a company at its outset took a risk, and the return on their shares, known as the dividend, rewards them for that risk. There is also a cost involved in lending money to a risky enterprise instead of leaving it to earn interest in the bank. The problem arises when the company becomes prosperous. According to the doctrine of usury, all debts must be repaid or cancelled; permanent interest is forbidden. But a modern public company's share capital entitles its owners not only to a perpetual return during the company's prosperity but also to permanent control of the company. This is usurious, whether we look at it practically, philosophically or religiously. Maynard (Lord) Keynes took the point when he wrote:

> For centuries, indeed for several milleniums, enlightened opinion held for certain and obvious a doctrine which the classical school (of Economics) repudiated ... I mean the doctrine that the rate of interest ...

* This chapter should be read in conjunction with Appendix 1.

constantly tends to rise too high, so that a wise government is concerned to curb it by statute and custom and even by invoking the sanctions of the moral law.[2]

The early history of usury takes us back to pre-Christian Greece and Rome. In the mediaeval Christian church the doctrine of usury lay at the heart of its canon law (see Appendix 1). The literature on usury is voluminous, and continued up to Adam Smith's day (1776). Adam Smith gave the doctrine fresh currency when he declared that the maximum interest rate should be five per cent.[3]

What has brought the financial and commercial system in our time under the general rubric of usury is not so much the high dividends paid on ordinary shares (we have seen that over the decade 1970–80 they were insufficient), as its payment in perpetuity, together with the accompanying right to exercise permanent control of the company and its policies. The result is to deny to the employees of a company, be they line operatives, foremen or managers, the right to participate in the formulation of corporate purpose in the company to which they may have devoted most of their working lives.

Thus the law has created a gulf between the shareholders and employees of a company, which in the ordinary way can never be bridged. It is indeed a case of 'them and us'. 'We', who do the work and make the company, retire and disappear at sixty or sixty-five. 'They', who do nothing but wait for their investment to bear fruit, are granted perpetual rights of control over 'our' company. This is the 'system' and it is under judgement. No such arrangement can last forever, for it is morally indefensible and opposed to the natural law. It is not enough to argue that the shareholders' permanent control of a company is necessary because someone has to be willing to bear the risks, and risk-taking justifies control. When recession hits a company, it is frequently the employees who are the first to suffer, and suffer heavily, by being turned out of their jobs. By comparison, the shareholders' risks are slight, and are in any case insurable through the holding of a mixed portfolio. There is little comparison between the impact of the loss of a job and the temporary loss of a dividend. One can be disastrous, the other inconvenient.

It is impossible to expect industrial relations to be normal while this disparity between the reward of capital and labour is allowed to persist. Again it must be emphasised that it is not the relative monetary reward that is unjust; on the contrary, if there is an injustice in reward it now appears to lie with the shareholder whose return, leaving aside capital gains, has steadily diminished until it barely covers the cost and the risk he bears by holding ordinary shares. What is usurious and vitiates industrial relations is the permanent nature of the equity. It is iniquitous to give control over an organisation dependent upon the daily co-operation of free men and women to absentee landlords from now until doomsday. We must choose between the perpetual equity and freedom, for the two are in the long run incompatible. Either capitalism will accept the demands of natural justice, or it will cease to exist and be replaced by a collectivist system likely to be a good deal worse.

A number of British and American companies have seen the danger and have acted to create employee shareholdings, either individually or through a trust fund. Since 1981 a British company may buy its own shares.[4] It can issue shares to trustees to be held for the benefit of the employees. Or it can allot money out of profits to trustees to be used for the purchase of the company's shares on the market. The trustees can then hold them against the time when the employee retires, when he receives his portion. Various methods are available for giving individual employees a financial interest in the company by means of a share in its equity, with help from the government in the way of tax remission or deferment. However, these schemes never go so far as to bring the company into the danger of being 'owned' by the employees or controlled through the employees' ownership of the company's shares. It is normally expected that control shall remain with the directors, acting on behalf of the absentee shareholders, rather than with the employees.

The concept of money lent to a company which can be converted by the lender into equity is familiar. What is required is the reverse use of this concept, whereby existing equity becomes subject to automatic redemption and repayment as a debt to the investor after an appropriate period.

Until the law has been changed to make equity shares in public companies subject to eventual termination (or conversion into preference stock), the shortest way to overcome the underlying discrepancy in purpose between the employees and the equity shareholders is to make the employees members of the company by setting up a trust fund on their behalf, and allowing them to exercise their individual right to vote according to the number of shares their interest in the trust fund represents.

What has to be done is to create a new concept of a public company, in which equity shares are regularly redeemed so that the company may eventually become a self-controlling and self-disciplining economic and social organism, fulfilling the corporate purposes set out in its memorandum. In other words, the public company must gradually be converted into a public trust whose directors are responsible for seeing that the terms of trust are carried out.

This solution calls for new institutional arrangements designed to canalise power and ensure accountability. These institutional arrangements include an extended annual general meeting, a social audit, and the appointment of a company referee. It also calls for representation at board level of the interests affected. What seems impossible to achieve under a system wedded to permanent control of the company by absentee shareholders, becomes possible and natural once that company has accepted the idea of eventual self-ownership.

This is a nettle that has to be firmly grasped. Half measures will fail. What caused the rejection of the recommendations of Lord Bullock's Committee of Inquiry on Industrial Democracy (1977) by employers and trades unions alike, was the dual role given to the trade union representatives on the company board and the union. These roles were widely felt to be incompatible. But once a company has accepted the obligation to 'give its employees every reasonable opportunity for their interests to be heard within the company' (see page 56) and a share in the equity, this difficulty is on its way to being overcome. The uncompromising pursuit of power on the part of unions and workers is a reaction to fear; fear that if and when the company is in difficulty or the victim of a takeover bid, the employees will be the first to suffer. Once the company has adopted the general purposes clause, a common purpose will have been defined and a binding commitment entered into with the workforce. What remains is to make this commitment visible and irrevocable by gradually vesting an increasing portion of the ordinary shares in the workforce, with full voting rights.

The purpose of gradually redeeming shares out of profits at their full market value is not to cause the individual shareholder to lose anything. It is to require him periodically to take the responsibility of re-investing his money in fresh risk-taking enterprise, and so to bring about what Adam Smith regarded as the key to national prosperity and full employment: the opportunity for a continual meeting in the 'marketplace' of willing sellers of labour with willing lenders of capital. Smith makes clear his view that an adequate and constant flow of capital is required to maintain employment. In *The Wealth of Nations* he is discussing the merits of the domestic market and is about to introduce the concept of 'the invisible hand':

> Upon equal, or only nearly equal profits, therefore, every individual naturally inclines to employ his capital in the manner in which it is likely to afford the greatest support to domestic industry and to give revenue and employment to the greatest number of people of his own country.[5]

To Smith an adequate flow of risk capital to the domestic market is a condition precedent for full employment. Redemption of share capital in public companies should increase that flow, while encouraging a growing sense of partnership between capital and labour through the introduction of an employees' trust fund in the company's shares.

10

*The Directors as Trustees**

In Chapter 8 we saw the public company being clothed with a general purposes clause with the object of gaining the moral assent of its employees and confirming and supporting the authority of its management and the position of the worker as a member of the firm. To underline the fact that the public company is not so much property as a living economic and social organism governed by natural law, we proposed in Chapter 9 that a public company's equity capital, in accordance with that law, should be redeemed over time.

As a result of the public company taking these two steps, the role of the directors will change. Instead of their fiduciary duties being solely concerned with the shareholders' interests, they will become responsible for carrying out the company's objectives as a whole, where, in the words of Eric Trist, 'The economic objective supplies the necessary condition but the social objective the sufficient condition for the survival and growth of the enterprise.'[1] This puts the directors into a position of trust, their trusteeship being to comply to the best of their ability with the corporate objectives in the general purposes clause of the memorandum.

The connection between trust and company is ancient. Professor F.W. Maitland, the famous jurist and historian (1850–1906), has traced it back at least four centuries.[2] Nor is there any doubt that before the passing of the limited liability acts in the middle of the nineteenth century, the directors of joint stock companies were regarded as trustees. In 1742, Lord Hardwicke decided in *Charitable Corporation v Sutton* that corporators were

* This chapter should be read in conjunction with Appendix 2.

trustees in equity for shareholders. This rule has been lost, directors having now come to be regarded as agents of the company rather than as trustees for the shareholders.[3] This is not surprising, seeing that the purpose of a company is presently confined in law to making a profit on behalf of the shareholders. But once a company has developed a corporate personality in which multiple and conflicting responsibilities arise, as in a nationalised railway or a privatised British Telecom, (both of which have virtual monopoly of the service) or as in large public companies, the directors of these and similar companies inevitably assume responsibilities of a wider nature. They include the customers, the employees, and the government, where the latter represents the corporations' source of capital or is its enabling authority. The need for trusteeship has now returned. It has already been noted (page 53) that the Companies Act 1985, section 309, requires directors 'to have regard to the interests of the company's employees in general' as well as those of their shareholders. A reason for introducing the clause was no doubt to reverse the decision in *Parke vs The Daily News*, 1962,[4] when the directors of the company were held to be acting *ultra vires* by compensating their employees on a winding-up with money not voted by the shareholders.

The clause as it reads gives no guidance to the question 'what are the employees' interests in general'. But the thrust of the clause is towards a concept of balance, or trusteeship. Indeed, section 309 expressly refers to the need for balance in its footnote, which reads: 'The directors will need to *balance* the interests of the various classes of members, the creditors and the employees.'

The duty of balancing conflicting claims in commercial affairs is not unknown to the law. In section 10 (1) of the Consolidating Restrictive Trade Practices Act 1976 it is expressly stated that the Restrictive Trade Practices Court shall determine

> that a restriction is not unreasonable having regard to the *balance* between those circumstances (i.e. of reasonable restriction) and any detriment to the public or to persons not parties to the agreement (being purchasers, consumers, or users of the goods produced or sold by such parties or persons . . .)

Here we have an external instrument, namely a court, charged with the duty of balancing claims in industry and commerce.

Admittedly section 309 of the Companies Act 1985 (consolidating the original section 46 in the 1980 Act) is only a step towards trusteeship, for it says nothing about the interests of consumers or the community. By inference it regards the company as consisting only of shareholders and employees, which is a one-sided concept of the responsibilities of a public company. Even this limited reference to the employees' rights is in practice controlled by the final phrase 'The power to enforce the duty lies within the company.' Any action to compel the directors to pay attention to their duty to consider the interest of their employees must therefore be taken by the majority of shareholders, and by no one else (such as an individual worker or his union), thereby effectively nullifying the section.

Nevertheless the introduction of the employees' interests into company law is a step forward and the first of its kind since 1862. It remains for the section to be widened so as to allow the duty towards employees to be enforced by the interested parties. (Another way to bring section 309 to life would be to make the employees members of the company: this will be dealt with in Chapter 11.)

In order to secure a true balance in corporate decision-making, what is needed is representation of the differing interests, including those of employees, on the board of directors. Here we enter a minefield of conflicting opinions. In West Germany the two-tier board enables the employees' voice to be heard as of right alongside that of the external shareholders. It appears likely that the European Economic Commission will eventually adopt the West German pattern for members of the EEC, with the addition of a Dutch variant providing for neutral members to be appointed with the consent of the remainder of the board up to one-third of the total number of board members.

Over against this we have the British one-tier board, whose protagonists argue that the representation of particular interests on a board cannot effectively be separated from joint responsibility for executive decisions. A third system is that of the American corporation with its monthly meetings of external directors, along with a few of the company's most senior executives, where policy decisions are submitted for approval by the executive to a body representing the shareholder interest. This system works well. But once employees become shareholders, the American board system is likely to become a forum for special pleading, as was feared if the West German supervisory board were to be imported into Britain.

The fact is that there is no possible solution to the problem of reconciling advocacy with decision-making in the board of directors so long as there exists an underlying conflict of interest between the parties. Only when a company has accepted a common purpose, and has written that purpose into its constitution, does it become possible to resolve the conflict of interest between the parties. For as long as a board is regarded as a place where opposing interests have to be reconciled, whether in a supervisory board as in West Germany, or in a single-tier board in Britain, so long will efficiency, with its need for rapid decisions, be sacrificed to advocacy, with its bias towards prolonging discussion in order to gain a point. When all members of a board are equally committed to an agreed common purpose, the diversity of interests they represent becomes an asset rather than a liability, and the particular kind of board best suited to the company's activities becomes a matter of convenience rather than of principle.

This transformation comes about not by the sacrifice of any one special interest but by the recognition that special interests, however deserving of advocacy, are in the end limited by the necessity of pursuing an overall purpose which binds and governs the whole. Every board member is equally responsible as a trustee for achieving the right overall balance in pursuance of the company's economic and social objectives. As an advocate he will put as forcibly as he can the views of his particular department, be it sales, finance, manufacturing or the designers and engineers, the unions, works councils, research or development. There being an accepted common purpose, the object of advocacy is not to defeat one's antagonist but to represent an interest faithfully, just as conflicting advocacy in a law court is designed to enable the truth to be revealed to judge and jury.

Once there is an agreed purpose in a public company, a second-tier board may be found a useful and, in a very large company, an essential device for making decisions, such as whether to invest in expensive new plant in a politically risky area where there are great natural resources. But the kind of supervisory instrument required in such a company need not be a board in the ordinary sense; it could be a committee of senior directors asked to formulate a policy for the full board's acceptance, after having listened to the arguments put forward by individual board members representing particular interests.

There will, of course, always be the possibility of a difference of opinion arising on the board as to the interpretation of its general purposes clause. This requires that there be someone outside the company to whom the board may look for an interpretation. Such a person would be appointed referee. The referee's normal role would be to settle any disputes arising as to the meaning of the company's stated objectives set out in its general purposes clause. Failing acceptance of the referee's recommendation, a fundamental difference of opinion on a board might have to go to a court for decision. But the referee should be given power to enforce his ruling, except where a third of the board is dissatisfied and regards the issue as one of principle, in which case the matter may have to go further. The rights of the parties in the company and the responsibilities of the directors to safeguard these rights will become the subject of a legal process, albeit informal in the first instance. In the event of a dispute involving the company and unions, the referee will already be familiar with both the facts and the personalities involved.

In order that the referee may familiarise himself with the company, he should have the right to attend board meetings and meetings of the works councils at his discretion. He would act as a longstop in any internal dispute over the interpretation of priorities laid down in the company's statement of general purposes.

What changes would be required in the constitution of the board? In a board with a unitary purpose, each of the departmental heads will speak for his particular constituency in much the same way as in the existing British unitary board. But there will be a number of outside directors, one or more of whom will represent the community locally and centrally. In the same way the consumers' interest will be represented by the board member in charge of sales, supported by an outside or part-time director whose function it will be to represent the consumers' interest. The proportion of outside to inside directors need not be fixed by law but could, on the Dutch and proposed EEC model, be one-third of the total directorate.

The present method of appointing directors, by recommendation to shareholders at the annual general meeting, need not alter. But in the responsible company the AGM will assume a larger role (as we shall see in Chapter 12), and representatives of the interests affected will have the right to attend and speak.

When employees are shareholders, they will automatically acquire the right to cast their vote in the appointment of directors, and where there is an employee share trust the appropriate number of votes represented by each employee's stake will be communicated to allow each employee to vote in the election of directors. This is the system successfully adopted by Sears Roebuck, whose employees own one-fifth of the company's equity.

11

Making Employees Shareholders

In 1986, fewer than fifteen per cent of British companies had introduced any form of share ownership scheme for their employees. Using corporate profits to encourage employees to buy and hold shares in their company has been looked on with disfavour by the 'City', in spite of some notably successful companies like Imperial Chemical Industries (ICI), which has issued shares to its employees since 1953, the John Lewis Partnership, whose shares have been held in trust for the firm's employees since 1929, and the Scott Bader Company whose employees were given the company by its founder, Ernest Bader, in 1957. Not only the City but the British trades unions have looked askance at employees becoming shareholders in their place of work. The unions have feared the creation of conflicting loyalties. There is also the argument that a working man should not be asked to add the risk of losing his money to that of losing his job. Finally, there is ideological dislike of the share ownership concept, the grounds for which were explored in Chapter 9.

In the USA, on the other hand, many employees have held shares in their companies since the 1950s, and there is both an impressive body of experience and a substantial record of its favourable results, involving some 200,000 companies.[1]

In 1977 the Bullock Report, with its proposal that trade union representatives should share in making board decisions as directors of public companies, raised so acutely the issue of conflicting loyalties, that the ownership of shares by a company's employees was made to seem innocuous by comparison. In 1978 the British Liberal party, for long committed to wider share ownership, was able to use its influence in a 'hung' parliament to introduce tax concessions by which income tax on employee share options was made deferrable. This was followed in 1979, 1980, and again in 1984, by important tax concessions on approved savings-related share option schemes.

As a result, a growing number of British companies, including BP, Marks & Spencer, Sainsburys and Mothercare, have introduced share schemes for their employees. In the older schemes, such as that pioneered by ICI, the employees were issued with shares individually and could sell them immediately, and half the workforce did. In the newer schemes there is a five- or seven-year pause on disposal before tax concessions apply fully.

A more radical scheme was that pioneered in the USA in 1916 by the giant Sears Roebuck firm (with its 300,000 employees). This consisted of the company's setting aside annually ten per cent of gross profits before tax and placing it with an employee share trust to buy the company's shares in the open market. The result over a period of years was to transfer some twenty per cent of the equity from shareholders to employees. In a big company like Sears Roebuck this represents a controlling interest, and the company has thereby gone a considerable way towards fulfilling the principle of redemption. It is also a company which has enjoyed the support of its employees over a long period and has been active in creating a role for itself as a good corporate citizen.

In Britain, the employee-owned National Freight Corporation resolved in October 1986 to tread the Sears Roebuck path by setting aside 12½ per cent of its pre-tax profits to enable its 26,000 employees to buy shares in their company on favourable terms, and so to retain internal control when the company eventually goes 'public'. Not surprisingly, the City of London is said to look with disfavour on the proposal, which breaches the City institutions' guidelines to industry (known as the Investment Protection Committee, or IPC) which are designed to limit employee participation in their company's shares.

The Sears Roebuck method has the advantage of helping to support the value of the company's shares, since there is always a ready buyer (the employees' trust) to intervene when the market falls. When the shares are bought by the employees' trust fund – which is a pension and savings fund – they are held with other securities and each individual employee is issued with a monthly statement showing the state of his account. In this way the individual employee has been made a partner in a trust fund which can, if the need arises, exercise a powerful influence on the annual general meeting.

The question of employee commitment has to be faced. Handouts do not of themselves create goodwill. They fail to provide the sense of personal achievement which human nature requires before it can be content. In Sears Roebuck the employees have been given the option to set aside five per cent of their pay to help build up more rapidly their stake in the trust fund. The British government's belated conversion in 1978–80 to tax concessions for company savings-related share option schemes makes possible a similar double approach to the strengthening of employee participation. In the USA, a company can transfer shares freely to its employees either by buying them on the open market (the Sears Roebuck method) or by the creation of new shares.* At the same time, it can encourage its employees to invest part of their earnings in a separate savings-related share option scheme. Together these schemes give the employee a sense of commitment lacking in either scheme separately. They express a joint interest, partly paid for by the employer and partly by the employee, in participation.

The fact that ordinary workers, once they have confidence in a company, will commit themselves financially, is underlined by the stiff entrance fee (£2,000) required of new employees in the successful Spanish Co-operative, Mondragon. Mondragon allows its employees to borrow the price of entrance into the company from the Mondragon Co-operative Bank, and it is only partly returnable to the employee when he leaves. The aim is to secure genuine commitment from the workforce in what is a self-owning partnership of 18,000 people working in one hundred or more associated companies.[2]

Separating the company's contribution of shares from that attaching to the employee through a savings-related share option scheme makes it clear that the former is a corporate gift to the whole body of workers, while the latter represents an opportunity – necessarily personal – for the individual employee to acquire a stake in the company on favourable terms. These two devices give the directors an opportunity to make a beginning with the repayment of the company's external debt and with the

* British law requires the latter route to be served. See the Companies Act 1985, sections 160 and 162.

transformation of the enterprise into a fully responsible company.

The question of how best to keep employee members informed of the company's progress admits of a variety of solutions. Sears Roebuck provides each employee monthly with a clearly-produced statement of his or her financial stake in the trust fund. Marks & Spencer issues with its annual report, in addition to the shareholder statement, a statement written for its employees. Attractively produced, it contains the minimum of financial information, the bulk of the report being devoted to the chairman's message, an account of the company's progress, its future development plans, its interest in community projects and the involvement of its employees in outside activities. It portrays the company as a group person with a conscience as well as a keen business sense. Marks & Spencer clearly thinks it worthwhile to take the trouble to explain to all its employees the social relevance of what they are doing as members of the company. The communication of information to employees needs to be a continuous rather than an occasional exercise, and at Marks & Spencer this is done by regular briefing sessions.

There is no simple answer to the question of how best to structure communication in a big company. In West Germany the works council is the preferred form. In Britain the trades unions generally prefer to handle communication through their own representatives, in order to ensure that their views are properly presented. To create a sense of common purpose which will win and retain the emotional assent of employees and cause them to modify the traditional attitude of suspicion of management is no easy task; nor can it be accomplished overnight.

One reason for defining the purposes of a company in its memorandum is to encourage indirectly this quality of emotional communication. When we place on record the purposes of an organisation by the adoption of a general purposes clause, we put the ordinary employee in a position to gauge the management's performance by its own avowed standards. When a company expresses an intention, as Shell and others have done, to pursue a policy of balance informed by a desire for justice, its management has issued a challenge to the employees to be governed by similar considerations. The individual may react at first with uncertainty and even hostility. If he is a shop steward or union official, he may fear to lose his identity. But in the long run the individual will respond, once he has become convinced that no threat is intended towards his own corporate loyalties, notably to his trade union. And when a company has finally convinced its employees, jointly and severally, that its aim is to pursue a path of balance by whatever light it can find, the role of the trade union will change, as it has changed in West Germany and in Japan. It will become less hostile in principle and more understanding in practice, with the end result of making greater efficiency possible through closer working relationships.

The future role of the trades unions is to develop, as they have done in West Germany, as agencies for the improvement of both the working conditions and the leisure opportunities of their members. The DGB (equivalent to the TUC in Britain) is already a major banker, hotelier, insurance agent, co-operative store, travel company and educator, and is constantly growing in social stature and influence. In Britain, the expanding positive role of trades unions has hardly been conceived. The unions thus have nothing to fear and everything to gain from radical reform of the public company on natural law principles. Co-operation is in all things the law of life, competition the law of death.[3]

However, we must not expect the trades unions to change or be converted overnight. Trade unionism is a corporate reaction to the lack of personal security felt in an industrial society. We get the trades unions we deserve. It is only when management shows itself to be consistently pursuing a course of balance informed by justice, and when the worker feels he has in a real way become a member of the firm, that the trades unions will change.

The average worker relies on his trade union to protect his individual interests. In return for the security this gives him, he hands over the negotiation of the terms and remuneration of his work to his trade union official or shop steward. For this to succeed he must give his allegiance to his working group, and in the continuing strength of that group lies the key to trade union power. Therefore, when a company wishes to improve its relations with its employees and is considering entering into a formal partnership with them by means of a share ownership scheme, it is advisable to begin with the group rather than the individual. The confidence of the workforce is built up by recognising their need for corporate loyalty rather than by appearing to undermine it. This is the value of the Sears Roebuck type of scheme, based on open market share purchases on behalf of the employees while at the same time encouraging a savings-related share option scheme based on the individual employee's contributions out of earnings. Both look forward to the eventual redemption of the company's external debt. While the gradual transfer of shares from the market to the employees, by whatever method, is a pledge to share future prosperity, its deeper purpose is the liberation of work. These two aims need to be held together, for the promise of prosperity is nothing without that of liberty.

12
Widening the Annual General Meeting

The average industrial worker in Britain and the USA wants to be free outside the job. He is not attracted by the prospect of becoming a company man. But the company nevertheless provides the setting for what is likely to be a significant aspect of his working life, the place where he expects to find the security and social respect he covets. Industrial psychologists are agreed that beyond a certain point more money is less important to the industrial worker than a sense of purpose. In the Hawthorne Experiment in the 1930s, Elton Mayo found that the worker's output was related to his quest for human significance, and that the desire to stand well with his fellows easily outweighed merely individual interest.[1]

A similar conclusion was reached after years of study by Professor Bakke of Yale University, who wrote that the average worker desires more money less than

> to play a socially respected and admired role, to win a degree of economic security customary among one's associates, to gain an increasing control over one's own affairs, and in all these to experience satisfying and predictable relations.[2]

It is this aspiration for social significance in the worker which makes the communication of corporate purpose important and justifies the effort of committing the company's aims to writing (Chapter 8). But how and when are these aims to be publicly proclaimed and reviewed?

The annual general meeting of the company in the past has been something of a formality. Accounts are presented and passed by the few shareholders who attend, retiring directors are re-elected or thanked for their services, auditors re-appointed, the chairman heard – sometimes venturing into the political arena – and, after a few questions and answers and a vote of thanks, the business brought to an end. It is a perfunctory affair as a rule.

Yet the AGM is the one occasion when a company can present itself clearly to the public eye and ear through newspaper reports and television. It is an opportunity for the company to display its real nature as a business enterprise, corporate citizen and social institution. If the communication of the purpose of the company is of primary importance, then the AGM is the right place and occasion. Let us take an example from the speech of the chairman of a British company noted for its social responsibility. This is part of what Lord Sieff had to say at the 1979 AGM of Marks & Spencer:

> We treat each member of our staff as an individual and with respect, keep them in the picture and encourage them to put forward their views, which are taken into account before decisions are made; the vast majority willingly accept the obligations and responsibilities as well as their benefits. Their attitude and involvement in the business are exemplary.

This statement was supported by a special report to the employees on the progress of the company, attractively and clearly presented. In a later passage of his speech the chairman dealt with the company's social responsibilities and its efforts to discharge them faithfully. But the primacy of customer relations was also stressed: 'For over 50 years the progress of our business has been based on upgrading the goods we sell and satisfying the changing needs of our customers.'

Here we see the AGM being used for its proper purpose: the communication of corporate attitudes as well as facts. In expressing concern for his customers, employees and the community as well as the shareholders, the chairman summed up in a simple way and in a few words the whole purpose of the company and the inter-relation of its parts.

What is still missing in the Marks & Spencer example is the sense of involvement on the part of those affected. The chairman's speech strikes the right note. In his annual report to employees for 1980 he writes of the company as 'your company' and asks for comments on his statement. But there is nothing analogous to a company parliament: the AGM is not a forum for the contrasting or conflicting views of staff, customers and community to be heard. The only benchmark against which Marks & Spencer's performance can be judged is the directors' own estimate of what their social responsibilities are. Giving away a million pounds a year is impressive, but as a percentage of gross profits it is marginal. This is not to belittle what Marks & Spencer has accomplished, but to say it falls short of the demands of democracy as applied to large-scale enterprise.

In the AGM of the future, there must be an opportunity for freely chosen representatives of the workers, consumers and the community to be present and to be allowed not only to ask questions but to speak about corporate policy and comment on the chairman's statement to the AGM.

The AGM is not the place for negotiation, whether about wages, conditions or pensions. It is the place, and perhaps the ideal place, for presentation of the company's overall policy in full view of those most affected by it. But for such a meeting to be constructive there first needs to be an agreed statement of purpose, or general purposes clause, as described in Chapter 8. The acceptance of this statement as a basic obligation on the directors will impose a like duty upon any who wish to comment at the AGM, establishing constructive terms of reference for that meeting. This is democracy: the expression of divergent views of elected representatives of special interest groups within a framework of agreed purpose which imposes its own order. Democracy is at its best when strong leadership – as in Marks & Spencer – is balanced by strong interest groups who can put their case effectively and have the right to do it publicly.

Admittedly, this will prolong the AGM. Instead of an hour and a half it may take six or more hours and may be spread over two days. But this need cannot be denied if reality is to be given to workers' participation in industry. If there is a time and place for the practice of industrial democracy it is in the company's AGM.

It is not only in the privacy of the works council, trade union, or board of directors that company policy in its broadest aspects needs to be considered and argued, but in the open. This is real democracy rather than so-called 'workers' control' of industry. The trouble with the latter expression is that it does not correspond to the facts of industrial life. Industry does not exist for the workers any more than for the shareholders; it exists to serve the consumer and the community, and this truth needs to be brought into the open and publicly enacted by each large public company at least once a year if we are to encourage democracy in industry in any meaningful way.

In the democratic society of the future the AGM of a large

company will be a public occasion. Representatives of the interests concerned will be invited to attend and speak. In this way the company will be protected from the syndicalist path of agreement between shareholders and employees at the expense of the consumer. Nationalised and privatised industries, in particular, will be required to allow time and place for a full public discussion of their corporate policies.

Questions put at the AGM by the appropriate consumer organisation would be answered by the board member responsible for consumer relations assisted by the external director with special responsibility for consumers (page 69). The main heads of discussion at the AGM should be reported in the financial press by the company, along with the company's financial results, as a matter of obligation. It is in the company's own interest to take the initiative in creating a more open style of AGM to allow genuine interest groups to express their views on company policy in the light of the company's declared objectives. Section 309 of the 1985 Companies Act and the growth of employee share trusts should eventually make employee representation at the AGM inescapable, and, if so, it is important to ensure that duly authorised representatives of other interests, notably those of the consumers and the community, are invited to keep a balance and to ensure that the debate is constructive. With minority groups able to buy shares and speak at the AGM, it is no longer possible to avoid discussion of political issues relating to company policy, such as doing business with South Africa. But whereas the responsible company is in a position to turn criticism at the AGM into positive channels, an ordinary company may have to suffer the indignity of being pilloried in public. The difference between them arises because there will be an agreed statement of corporate purpose in the responsible company to which reference can be made. In this way, criticism of the board over a particular issue can be treated by the chairman as a constructive contribution to the directors' task of finding the right balance in policy. The exact area of corporate accountability will, however, need to be clearly defined and limited beforehand, and this points to the creation of a new instrument for use at the AGM, namely the social audit.

13
The Social Audit

Each year companies are required to submit their accounts for inspection and audit by a qualified firm of accountants. In this way the shareholders satisfy themselves that the company has been properly conducted and its accounts give a true picture of the company's affairs. These accounts are presented at the annual general meeting for adoption, and are open for discussion. The accountants will be invited to attend and speak at the AGM.

There is no corresponding audit of the non-financial aspects of a company's affairs, no independent appraisal of a company's performance in relation to its employees or its customers or the community of which it is a member. These aspects of corporate accountability are dealt with, if at all, in the chairman's speech. It is usual to thank the employees for their services and to make some reference to the company's progress in meeting the needs of its customers. But that is as far as it goes, unless, like Marks & Spencer, a separate annual report is issued to employees in which the company's activities are reviewed in all their ramifications, social as well as economic.

Now that the directors of a company are required to have regard to the interests of the company's employees as well as of its shareholders (section 309 of the Companies Act 1985), there would seem to be a clear case for the company's annual report to refer to those interests. This is all the more necessary in companies which have set up employees' share trusts under one of the various schemes now recognised and qualifying for tax relief or tax deferment. Just as the shareholders expect their interest in the company to be satisfied by a wide-ranging report from the chairman at the AGM, covering the company's present and future prospects, so will the company's employees come to expect their general interests to be considered and reported upon so that questions may be raised and answered, doubts revealed and dispelled and corporate policy be submitted to constructive criticism.

All this calls for some independent appraisal of the company's social performance, or a social audit. Such an audit would require professionally-trained people who would look at and report upon the company's performance in its social and human aspects, just as the auditors look at the company's financial performance and report upon it. This is not to be confused with the efficiency audit conducted by a government body or official, or by management consultants.

The social auditors could be drawn from, among other places, the social science faculties of universities, including colleges like Nuffield, Oxford and the Tavistock Institute, London. Some large British companies like Shell have already begun to do this, as we saw in Chapter 8. In the Netherlands, a leading producer of steel, Hoogovens, instituted a social audit in 1969 as part of a collective agreement with labour. This took the form of a report now distributed annually to all personnel, which forms the basis of subsequent discussion with the trades unions. The largest private company in India, Tata, instituted a social audit in 1979, in their Iron and Steel Division. Three distinguished persons, a judge, a former member of parliament and a professor of labour relations, were appointed by the board to draw up the terms of reference in agreement with them and to conduct the audit.

Prior to commissioning the social audit, Tata Steel altered its articles of association, adding a general purposes clause (3A) similar to that suggested in Chapter 8. The terms on which the social auditor were appointed read as follows:

> To examine and report whether, and the extent to which, the company has fulfilled the objectives contained in Clause 3A of its articles of association regarding its social and moral responsibilities to the consumers, employees, shareholders, society and the local community.

The first report of the social auditors was published in 1980 and covers all aspects of the business in its sixty-five pages. The auditors are, in places, sharply critical of the company, notably in regard to the control of pollution; but on the whole their assessment is positive and favourable. They comment upon the fact that dividends 'appear to be somewhat meagre' and suggest the government be approached for permission to increase them, a suggestion with which the directors complied! The report makes clear what was already known in Indian government and business circles: that Tata is among the leading companies in the practice of social responsibility.

The alteration of Tata's articles to include a general purposes clause, and the subsequent creation of a social audit, followed a ten-day conference on the social responsibility of business convened by Jayaprakash Narayan in New Delhi in 1965 and opened by Mr Shastri, the Indian Prime Minister. It was attended by leading Indian industrialists, including senior representatives of Tata. Professor Allan Flanders and I were delegates from Britain and we helped draw up a 'Declaration on the Social Responsibilities of Business', which was subsequently adopted by the Trusteeship Movement of India and published along with the proceedings.[1]

The original expression 'social audit' has been adopted by at least one management consultant in Britain to describe something different, a structured process of managerial self-examination. This is not so much an audit as an internal tool of management. Nor is the idea new to the nationalised sector of industry in Britain. In the report of the Parliamentary Select Committee on the Nationalised Industries, 1968, Professor W.A. Robson is quoted as urging the need for efficiency audits in the nationalised industries. In the course of his evidence he pointed out that these industries are unique in escaping any kind of constitutional control through audit. Not surprisingly the chairmen of the nationalised industry boards objected to any outside surveillance of their managerial competence and nothing was done at the time. This is mentioned because a clear distinction needs to be made between the idea of a social audit undertaken at the request of the board of a company, and the creation of a Public Industries Audit Office with compulsory powers of oversight.

The reason for distinguishing the idea of a social audit from that of an efficiency audit is that the former is intended to enable informed discussion of a company's policies to take place at its AGM. There needs to be available an independent opinion if the democratic process is to work constructively in its industrial context. Once a company has publicly recognised that it has social as well as financial obligations and has sought to define these (if only to limit them), it becomes a logical step to set up a social audit from time to time – not necessarily annually – in order to show publicly that it is acting within the definition of its corporate purposes as set out in its general purposes clause.

If public companies fail to grasp the nettle of occasional independent appraisal of their overall policies by competent observers, they will find the job being done for them, and done in a way that may be damaging to their interests. In Britain, the Public Interest Research Centre in 1973 established a subsidiary known as 'Social Audit', with the purpose of examining and reporting upon the social conduct of selected companies. 'Social Audit Report 3' dealt with Tube Investments in a sharply critical manner and was undertaken without co-operation from the management. Report 4 reported unfavourably on the financial empire of Sir Denys Lowson and its effect on a mining community in Kentucky, USA. Report 5 criticised Cable & Wireless Ltd for covering up losses amounting to over £2 million and showed how such concealments are facilitated by present auditing and accounting standards.[2] In default of public companies commissioning their own social audits, it is hardly surprising that outside bodies have begun to enter the field. If a company like Tube Investments attracted a hostile social assessment, it may be because that company failed to take positive action to create its own social audit in time.

The institution of a social audit presupposes that management has sufficient confidence in itself to welcome an occasional impartial outside appraisal. Efficient management will always be anxious to learn anything that can help it to become even more efficient. By initiating a social audit, management puts itself into a position to ensure that in any subsequent discussion with the interested parties a balanced view will be maintained and the relevant facts accurately stated. As experience accumulates and the use of a social audit becomes general, the auditors will develop a body of comparative data on which to build an increasingly professional assessment, enabling standards to be set and helping management to improve its performance through comparison with the social practices of other companies.

Whence will the supply of social auditors come? They may come from the large number of directors of companies who now retire at sixty or sixty-five at the height of their powers. Their experience and independence will ensure that the social audit is dealt with constructively and not with a view to finding fault. The social expansion of the large public company requires sympathetic monitoring in the interests of achieving excellence and balance, and the social auditors will be in a position to compare the company's performance with its declared purposes as well as with other companies.

In Chapter 10 (page 69) reference was made to the appointment of a company referee chosen by the board, with the specific duty of interpreting the company's general purposes clause when a dispute arose as to its meaning. This person, who would attend board meetings as an observer, could also perform a useful role in organising the occasional social audit and ensuring its independence and balance. He would in effect fill the role of ombudsman to the company.

An alternative suggestion put forward by the Institute of Chartered Secretaries in the wake of the Guinness scandal (January 1987) is that the company secretary be required by law to monitor agreements made by the board as 'Compliance Officer'. This raises a problem of conflicting loyalties. It would be hard for a line officer of the company to maintain his independence, whereas the company referee, although appointed by the board, would be in an independent position, his responsibility being to advise the company on compliance with its declaration of purpose.

14

The Reform of Nationalisation: A Missed Opportunity

In no section of the business community is there a greater need for clear purpose, adequate representation of the consumers, employees and the community, and a public forum for discussion and appraisal, than in the nationalised industries. These great, monopolistic concerns, which the post-war British Labour government created, include the Coal Board (1946), British Rail (1947), the Electricity Authority (1947), the Gas Boards (1948) [privatised in 1986] and the Steel Industry (1951).

When the nationalised industries were created in the 1940s, control of their boards and the appointment of their chairmen was given to the cabinet minister responsible. This ensured a continuing political element in the direction of these vital services. It also entailed a lack of continuity in policy, as one government succeeded another at intervals of four to five years. Finally it made it difficult, if not impossible, to achieve the desirable level of decentralisation.[1]

In order to solve the problems of the nationalised industries, two related principles have to be reconciled: those of liberty and authority, expressed respectively in the right to representation and the right to manage. When powers are given to a cabinet minister to represent several interests in a nationalised company simultaneously, the right of those interests to be consulted and heard is curtailed and stultified. The minister cannot possibly represent the gas or electricity consumer at the same time as he represents the views of the Treasury. Nor can he speak for the consumer and at the same time announce a high wages policy. What is needed is to create a representative institution, or responsible company, in which the differing interests are allowed to make their distinctive contributions and to be heard by a board responsible in the end for making policy, subject only to the normal financial disciplines exercised by the shareholders of a public company. In this way alone can there be hope of a continuous policy for the nationalised industries, while without managerial continuity there cannot be a serious possibility of raising morale among the workforce, even to the extent achieved in well-managed sectors of the private economy. The generally disappointing response of the labour force under nationalisation is a sad by-product and commentary on the lack of continuity in the policies pursued and the lack of independence of its management.

In addition to representation of the separate interests at board level, there needs to be a continuous public process of discussion and review. Something like an extended annual general meeting is needed where representatives of the consumers, employees and community interests may attend and speak, and have their comments and questions recorded and answered by the board.

It is important that discussion of policy in a nationalised (or privatised) industry should be seen by the public to be fair and to take into account the legitimate concerns of all interests affected. Since 1945, the representation of consumers' interests in the nationalised coal, electricity supply, gas and railway industries has been in the hands of forty-four consultative committees which work within the framework created by the Nationalisation Acts of 1945–1950.

In 1981 the Department of Trade issued a consultative document: *Consumers' Interests and the Nationalised Industries*. It frankly admitted the shortcomings inherent in a network of advisory committees without executive power or direct representation on the nationalised industry boards. 'There is a gap to be bridged between customer and nationalised industry' (section 27). The solutions proposed included reducing the number of advisory bodies, placing greater emphasis on customer complaints, establishing closer liaison between the advisory councils, improving communications to make sure the public knows its rights and its representatives and introducing an efficiency audit.

What is wrong with these proposals? Firstly, they do not give the consumers a voice on the board which could be heard, for example, when higher wages were being demanded by the workforce. They do not give the consumer bodies the right to appoint their own representatives on the national councils. The departmental ministers retain the control and the initiative. They appoint the members but only pay the chairman. The result is that the secretary to the industry consumer council is a bureaucrat working within an establishment setting. This makes it unlikely that complaints will be dealt with in a spirit of urgency and determination, as the writer discovered for himself when he formed the Reading Passengers' Association in 1965 and dealt directly on behalf of its 300 members with the top management of British Rail over the heads of a supine and spineless official consumer council.

If there is to be genuine democracy in the nationalised or privatised industries, there must be a framework of reference which the public can grasp and understand; not a complex act of parliament which is a closed book to the layman, but a simple statement of corporate purpose like the Shell statement. What is needed is a general purposes clause (outlined in Chapter 8) which sets out simply and clearly what the purpose of the gas or electricity supply or coal industry is, and how its differing and often conflicting responsibilities – to its consumers, employees, financial masters and the environment – are intended to relate to one another in practice.

A general purposes clause is also necessary to determine the scope and limits of the extended annual general meeting which every nationalised or privatised industry should be required to hold in full public view and with representatives of the employees, consumers and the community attending with the right to speak and ask questions. This requires the appointment of outside directors who can answer for the special interest they represent on the board in support of the full-time directors who will speak for their respective departments, be it sales, service, finance, research and development, manufacturing or design.

A thorough and detailed review of the nationalised industries was mounted in 1967 by a select committee of parliament whose report is to be found in three volumes published in 1968.[2] When the heads of the nationalised industries were called before the select parliamentary committee, they spoke of the confusion created by their conflicting obligations (para 117). The chairman of the Electricity Council said that during his time of office there had never been a comprehensive, consistent or coherent policy (para 118). The chairman of British European Airways said there was no clear-cut policy. The chairman of the National Coal Board put it this way: 'I have been at the Coal Board for six years only. I have had four ministers, three parliamentary secretaries.

If there is one thing you want in an industry like ours, with the largest payroll in Western Europe, it is some consistency.' (vol. 11, para 510)

The select committee summed up the evidence in the following passage:

The committee concludes, to put it simply, that ministers have largely done the opposite of what parliament intended. They were supposed to lay down policies but not to intervene in the management of the industries in implementing those policies. In practice, until recently, they have given the industries very little policy guidance, but they have become closely involved in many aspects of management. Much of the former, the committee believes, has sprung from confusion about responsibilities and about purposes. (para 40)

The difficulty a responsible minister faced under the Morrisonian type of nationalisation was described by the select committee in paragraph 89 of its report:

Ministers are responsible to a body which expresses three separate and frequently conflicting interests: namely the interest of the consumers of the goods and services provided by the industries, the interest of the tax payers, and the interests of the board's employees.

The select committee might have added a fourth interest, namely that of the local communities in which the nationalised industries operate. The sheer drabness of many of our colliery towns is enough to account for bad labour relations in the mines and should certainly be taken into review by the Coal Board. D.H. Lawrence has given a brilliant description of life in a coal mining area:

Now though perhaps nobody knew it, it was ugliness which really betrayed the spirit of man, in the nineteenth century. The great crime which the moneyed classes and promoters of industry committed in the palmy Victorian days was the condemning of the workers to ugliness, ugliness, ugliness; meaningless and formless and ugly surroundings, ugly ideals, ugly religion, ugly hope, ugly love, ugly clothes, ugly furniture, ugly houses, ugly relationship between workers and employers. The human soul needs actual beauty even more than bread.[3]

A social audit (Chapter 13) should be required of every nationalised and privatised concern as a matter of course. We saw in the previous chapter that at the hearings of the parliamentary select committee objections were raised to having an audit committee examine management's record. Where an audit is in the nature of an inquest, the objection is understandable. But this can and should be avoided.

Within the limits set by the general purposes clause, an extended general meeting and the social audit provide the basis for an open and public dialogue annually between the board, its employees and the public. The minister should intervene only in order to make the position of the government clear in his representative capacity as the financial stakeholder. He should not be allowed to interfere in managerial matters affecting the industry any more than the ordinary shareholders of a public company may do.

In managing a public company or a nationalised or privatised industry there is no perfect solution of the continuous tension between liberty and authority. The best that can be done is to make the purpose of the institution explicit, provide the opportunity for a fair and free expression of informed opinion by the interested parties, and invest management with the authority necessary to execute policy once it has been agreed in principle. This is the way of the responsible company, and is what is needed by way of reform of the nationalised (and privatised) industries.

These suggestions are not only the result of hindsight. The superficial nature of the original legislation should have been clear to anyone who thought about the matter. At the time the legislation was going through parliament (1947–1950), the writer was in touch with Herbert Morrison, then Home Secretary and Deputy Prime Minister and generally regarded as the main architect of nationalisation. Through a mutual friend, Dr S.C. Leslie (head of the Treasury's information division), Herbert Morrison asked to see an advance text of *The Future of Private Enterprise,* which I was then writing. We met several times over lunch, when I urged the Home Secretary to set up a board in each industry genuinely representative of the consumer and employee interests as well as of the government. I thought these boards should be allowed their independence and given extensive powers of self-direction and freedom from day-to-day ministerial influence. I kept a note of our conversations. One, dated 23 October, 1950, reads:

I told Herbert Morrison I thought his policies would result in concentrating power in the nationalised sector in the hands of the minister instead of creating a balanced power structure in which the employees, consumers, government and local communities would all have a place where they could make their distinct contribution to the formulation of adequately balanced programmes and policies for the industry. Herbert (Morrison) replied that there was no time to think out the theory of nationalisation; the government were pledged to take action and must make the best job of it they could, and leave it to others to put right what was found wrong.

In the event, nationalisation was introduced in such a hurry that in the case of the coal industry there was in the Ministry of Mines no blueprint of any kind; not even the outline of a plan. Everything had to be improvised in order to meet the government's deadline. The result was to combine the worst of two worlds: over-centralisation, and the continued employment of the old colliery managers with their mixed record, with the resulting exclusion of the miners from participation in the reorganisation of the mines. We are still paying the price of our failure to place the nationalised industries on a firm foundation of public responsibility and public accountability. Unfortunately what was missing in the 1950s is still missing in the 1980s, as the initial steps taken to privatise industries previously nationalised do not appear to be based on any sounder philosophy of the company than the hit-or-miss policies of the past. What the industrial experience of Britain has shown in the last thirty years is that goodwill and self-restraint by the workforce of a nationalised industry cannot be presumed. It must be earned.

15
Creative Enterprise

There are one and one-third million small businesses in Britain, employing some five million workers. In West Germany there are half as many again, in Japan five times, and in the USA ten times as many. We need to double the number of small businesses in Britain. We could employ another two to three million people in this way. How can it be done? We do not know. What we do know is that it cannot be done without the help of the big companies. It is they who possess the experience and managerial skills, the technical know-how, the resources, the premises and facilities, and the access to fresh capital. It is largely the big company, forced to shed labour to remain competitive, that has created the problem of structural unemployment, and it is the big company which should help in finding the solution. Moreover, the public company has become a powerful agent of social change in the closing years of the twentieth century, and its constitution should begin to reflect that fact.

We need to discover a new relationship between the large enterprise and its resources on the one hand, and the local community and its resources on the other. The object must be to set people free to work in and for their locality, partly in public works, such as the regeneration and improvement of the housing stock, and in the creation of local amenities, and partly by starting fresh businesses. Responsibility for public works will be taken by local authorities, and executed by special corporations similar to the Allegheny Conference on Community Development which rebuilt the city of Pittsburgh in the 1950s. The small enterprise will be assisted by organisation on the lines of the Local Enterprise Trusts, formed by the initiative of a number of outstanding British companies, including ICI, Pilkingtons and

Marks & Spencer. These are broadly based local groups which help in establishing new businesses by giving expert advice about premises, facilities and finance and, when necessary, lending their employees. To this must be linked the provision of appropriate banking services. The clearing banks in Britain have grown too large and centralised to give an adequate service to the small man, especially when he is starting a business. Graham Bannock[1] has shown that, by contrast, in West Germany the local co-operative banks account for two-thirds of all loans to small businesses, and act towards them with a sympathy generally lacking in Britain. Active support for the financial needs of small businesses also lies behind the success of the Japanese in fostering a large and flourishing small business sector.

In his Ashridge Lecture, C.C. Pocock, then chairman of Shell, described some of the ways in which big business could help small firms:

> I believe there is a role for even more positive help. For example, by credit or financial pump-priming for the small operator while he is establishing himself; assignment of a specialist to help with accounting and costing; help to an innovator in his early years with a view to a lasting relationship later. All of us in large industry will have ideas which have been developed in-house but put on the back burner because there was no prospect of early development. Most of us will know of products which are of commercial interest but not worth developing in a large company. Why not encourage smaller people to develop these products against a purchase order for their early production? Why not encourage a retiring employee to take an idea with him, develop it, hiring people for the purpose, and sell us back the product for market development?[2]

In the early days of the industrial revolution, before limited liability had been invented, the entrepreneur, or enterpriser, of necessity took a heavy personal risk in starting an enterprise. In his famous dictionary (1755), Dr Johnson defines the enterpriser as 'a man of enterprise, who undertakes great things; one who engages himself in important and dangerous designs.' Often the enterpriser founded his business to produce and market his own invention with the help of his friends.

In our time, industry is again being required to undertake great and dangerous things: to put social responsibilities high on its list of priorities; to improve its product; to involve its work-force in a partnership of endeavour; to pursue excellence and to help create new employment opportunities. None of this is likely to happen while the public company is looked upon as shareholders' property and its workforce excluded from membership of the company.

The plea made in this book is for a new corporate philosophy. We need to see the company as an agent for social improvement as well as a money-making machine. The appeal must not only be to the self-interest of the employee, but to his sense of responsibility as a member of a working community which is itself a part of a larger community.

Throughout this book examples have been given of British companies which have embraced the concept of the responsible company – Shell, BP, Marks & Spencer, ICI, Pilkingtons. In a few cases entire control has been transferred to the firms' employees – the John Lewis Partnership (1929), Scott Bader (1957), the National Freight Corporation (1982). Abroad we have had examples of responsible companies before us for years. In Germany, the Karl Zeiss Foundation achieved worldwide acclaim for its commitment to its workforce (sole owners of the business since 1896), research in optics, based in the University of Jena, and for its generous constitution, perfect of its kind, which even the Russian occupiers of East Germany fifty years later found themselves unable to destroy. The Zeiss Constitution, by which Karl Abbe gave the firm to his employees, is still the most comprehensive and successful of its kind known to the writer.*

In Chapter 11 we discussed the Sears Roebuck (USA) employees' trust fund established in 1916. In Spain, we noted the example of the successful Mondragon Co-operative. All these companies have been successful commercially. All have established close working relations with their employees, all are profitable. The John Lewis Partnership, entirely employee-owned, has been expanding for many years at twice the rate of its competitors. Why have these and other good examples not been followed?

The answer is plain, although not reassuring. The usurious outlook, which treats a company as shareholders' property instead of as a living organism, simply cannot see the daylight.

* In 1946 Sir Stafford Cripps asked for a translation of the Zeiss Constitution, and a shortened English version was published as an appendix in *The Responsible Company* (1961) and its predecessor *The Future of Private Enterprise* (1951).

The 'City' view, and its preoccupation with short-term gains, is alien to the whole concept of industrial and commercial partnership over a long time span.

The measures proposed in this book – a general purposes clause in the memorandum of public companies, the gradual redemption of equity capital, making directors trustees, enfranchising the employees, creating an extended annual general meeting, appointing a referee and establishing a social audit – are all legislative steps which would be unnecessary if industry were free of the usurious outlook. That outlook is now out of date.

Let us look for a moment at the American industrial scene. The largest company in the USA, if not in the world, is General Motors. In January 1972 an article about the company in the American journal, *Fortune*, said:

> The automobile industry in general, and General Motors in particular, is under fire on a dozen fronts ... Most G.M. officers now tend to place the country's social and environmental problems high on their list of the biggest challenges facing the company ... the 'Campaign to make General Motors Responsible' proposed that G.M. elect three directors representing the public and create a stockholder committee on corporate responsibility. The concern voiced by a number of large institutional investors about the issue raised by Campaign G.M. was, says one G.M. director, 'an eye-opener'. The board soon thereafter established a Public Policy Committee made up of five outside directors including G.M.'s retired vice chairman and elected the Rev. Leon Sullivan, a tough-minded black founder of job training centres, to the board. It was the public policy committee that suggested that G.M. create its new scientific advisory committee. This group ... has been examining G.M.'s influence on society and has proposed some large changes.

Here we see the largest of American enterprises facing up to the social implications of its business; its total impact on the community. If more companies were like G.M. and if more British companies had followed the lead of Zeiss, Sears Roebuck and the John Lewis Partnership, legislation would be unnecessary. It is the concentration on short-term gain, the usurious view, that make legislation inevitable.

The great question remains. Can Britain afford a less participative form of enterprise than its competitors in Europe, Japan and the USA? Or has the time come for the country which led the first industrial revolution to lead the industrialised nations a second time, by returning to those mutual aid principles which are also the principles of the natural law? For Britain, time is running out. We need the responsible company now.

APPENDIX 1

*A Note on Usury**

The problem of usury is one with which humans have grappled from ancient time. Plato forbade usury in the 5th Book of the Laws, while Moses and the Prophets condemned it in the name of Jehovah. The Law of the Twelve Tables limited interest in Republican Rome to one per cent, and even this was prohibited later by Julius Ceasar. Plutarch tells us that Solon pronounced an amnesty on debts to rid Athens of usury, while Agis burnt the usurers' books in Laconia for the same reason. Yet usury continued to exist and continues to this day. Rightly does St Paul call the love of money the root of all evil. Like bindweed it springs up perennially and, unless continually rooted out, overgrows the most flourishing commonwealth, binding to destroy.

From the dim light of ancient history it is with relief that we pass to the great body of mediaeval teaching on usury, known as the canon law, the first systematic attempt to apply the principles of right and wrong to the economic sphere. The canon law, with the fully evolved doctrine of usury at its centre, came to maturest expression in the fifteenth century, but already at the Council of Vienna (1311) usury had been prohibited by the church, and the next century saw this prohibition embodied not only in canon but also in civil law of Western Europe.

According to the mediaeval view, usury is present in any contract or loan which calls for a fixed rate of gain without corresponding risk to the lender. To lend money on security and to demand interest as well as the return of the principal is usury. On the other hand, to share risks, as in a partnership, is not usury. Annuities are free of usury for the reason that there is a gamble on the life of the borrower, hence a risk to the lender.

* This appendix should be read in conjunction with Chapter 9.

The mediaeval prohibition of usury was based on the view that money is a consumable like wheat or wine, in which use and consumption are inseparable (unlike houses, land or tools in which use is distinct from consumption). It follows that a contract for the loan of money necessarily involves alienation of the property in the money and its consumption by the borrower, in return for which privilege the borrower undertakes to repay a like (but not the identical) sum on a given date in the future. This promise of repayment may be secured by the deposit of bonds or other assets. No further payment may be demanded by the lender under canon law, since it belongs to the nature of lending in a Christian community to be free and liberal, always providing the risk of loss is adequately secured. To stipulate for the repayment of more than the principal under such circumstances was held to be contrary both to natural law and Christian revelation. In accordance with this theory, usury was officially defined in England in the Act of 1495 (II Henry VII, Ch. 8) as 'taking for the same loan anything more besides or above the money lent by way of contract or covenant at the time of the same loan, saving lawful penalties for the non-payment of the money lent.' It was a natural further step to substitute for the penalty a fixed amount of damages reckoned periodically, and this gave rise to interest.

Thus the term 'interest' was originally used to denote a penalty exacted for non-repayment of a loan on the date due. The penalty was usually fixed at an amount equivalent to the original debt (see Ashley: *Ecclesiastical History*, Part II, p. 399). Mediaeval theologians, including Thomas Aquinas, accepted the justice of interest as compensation for non-repayment of a loan, provided the damage was real and not fictitious. This principle was termed *damnum emergens*, literally 'injury appearing', and the proof of damage lay with the lender.

Where, however, loans were made for productive use rather than for immediate consumption, the lender might feel it a hardship to deprive himself of the opportunity to employ his resources in other profitable ways, such as in improving his own property. And so the canonists evolved a second justification for interest on loans which they called *lucrum cessans*, literally 'gain ceasing'. As the opportunities and facilities for investment increased, so the potential sacrifice of advantage in lending money without interest grew. True, Aquinas (and after him Luther) pointed out that since all life is uncertain, there can be no certain fixed gain which is capable of advance determination. But granting the possibility, Aquinas admitted the justice of the claim to interest, as compensation for certain loss. Hence his successors found themselves driven by the facts of economic progress and the improvement in banking methods to admit that money might be profitably employed with certainty and that money lent might, therefore, justifiably carry a rate of interest to compensate the lender for the loss of opportunity his loan entailed, as well as to indemnify him against non-payment.

These two mediaeval justifications for taking interest on loans may be re-stated in modern terms as payment to the lender for risk and cost. In both cases the onus of proof lay with the lender, failing which the borrower was entitled to borrow free of interest. The taking of interest could be justified only in the case of an unsecured loan, and even then could be no higher than the real risk to the lender. As for the cost of lending, mediaeval practice did not recognise abstinence as entitling the lender to a reward; but only the certainty of loss to the lender through being deprived of other uses for his surplus where gain was certain and capable of advance calculation. Again, the onus of proof lay with the lender.

Generally speaking, religious opinion after the Reformation did not differ from that before it in its condemnation of usury. It has already been noted that Luther held the strict mediaevalist view against usury. It is among the sixteenth-century Catholic theologians, such as the Jesuit Molina, that we find the first signs of revolt against the strict canonist view. In England, Henry VIII had legalised usury in 1545 by permitting loans carrying interest up to ten per cent per annum. This act was repealed in 1552. But in 1571 a fresh act of parliament was passed. It provided that all contracts for payment of interest of over ten per cent were to be null and void. Creditors were denied redress at law, even on their claims to interest at less than ten per cent. Interest was thus still nominally outlawed. But the act of 1571 changed the climate of thought – or, rather, it recorded in legal form the change of thought already current – by distinguishing between interest above and below ten per cent. Before 1571 all fixed interest had been held *prima facie* to be usurious unless falling within certain clearly allowable categories, of which the principal were rent charges, commercial partnerships (in which loss was shared as well as gain), annuities, fees for delay in payment and voluntary payments. After 1571, an arbitrary line was drawn between interest above and below ten per cent. Although the protection of the law was still withheld from the creditor, the watershed between mediaeval and modern practice had been crossed. From now on the distinction between what was allowable and what was not became one of degree, not one of kind, and with this change of emphasis the scriptural basis for the prohibition of usury was overthrown. R.H. Tawney calls the change of thought momentous, and asks if any intellectual revolution could be more profound than one which substituted expediency for a supernatural criterion.[1]

The part played by Calvin in this historic break with the tradition of the church and the views of theologians has been misunderstood. Calvin dealt with usury 'as the apothecary deals with poison', wrote a contemporary. But his carefully qualified approval of interest in certain circumstances was wrested by his eager followers, the bankers and merchants of the Low Countries, into an unqualified approval of the commercial practices then growing up. In this respect, Calvin was no more a Calvinist than Erastus was an Erastian. Both are victims of their followers.

To what extent does the Bible account of usury support the mediaeval doctrine in its full elaboration? There are only twelve references in the Bible to usury and they are all found in the Old Testament, except for the double account in the Gospels of the Parable of the Talents, where Our Lord is clearly not expressing a moral view of usury but using a well-known daily fact of life to illustrate the truth that spiritual gifts must either be used or lost.

Usury in the Bible means the taking of interest in any form in return for the loan of money or goods. To Ezekiel, as to David, the just man is 'he that hath not given forth upon usury neither hath taken *any* increase'. In the Mosaic law, usury is a crime as heinous as theft or adultery. In ancient Rome usurers were punished by exacting as a penalty four times the principal sum, compared with only twice the principal sum in the case of restitution for theft.

The Mosaic prohibition of usury rests upon three passages – Exodus XXII 25, Leviticus XXV 35, and Deuteronomy XXIII 19. The last-mentioned permits usury on loans to the stranger, a distinction not found in Exodus or Leviticus. The apparent inconsistency is, however, resolved by the definition of the stranger in Leviticus XIX, 34, 'the stranger that dwelleth with you shall be unto you as one born among you.' The stranger from whom interest may be taken is evidently the stranger living in a foreign land (Deuteronony XV 3), *not* the stranger living in the midst. Nor is this distinction a quibble. To lend freely to one's neighbour, whether stranger or not, was a charitable and communal obligation then as now. But to lend to a stranger living in a foreign community, which recognised no common ties and was not bound by the Mosaic law, meant, in the prevailing society, undertaking a considerable risk. Loans within the primitive community could be secured either on the person or the land of the borrower, subject, in the case of Israel, to the periodic or jubilee release provided by the Mosaic law. But loans outside the community could not be secured and interest (called usury) was therefore permitted. In the primitive state of Old Testament society, no distinction was drawn between usury and interest because as a practical matter risk did not arise within the community, and cost to lender was incalculable even if it existed. Risk might even be negative; that is to say, it might be safer to lend than to withhold a loan. Prince Kropotkin tells the story in his *Mutual Aid* of an Eskimo ceremony at which those who prosper by trading periodically distribute their surplus to the members of the tribe as a safeguard against future misfortune. In a moment of emergency, neither a blizzard nor a polar bear can be bought off with a present of money. In such conditions, safety lies in charity, and to dispose of one's surplus in good time is prudence.

Thus the mediaeval doctrine of usury, while resting on the Biblical prohibition, greatly elaborates the justification for interest found in Deuteronomy XXIII 19. A fresh reading of the Bible passages dealing with usury would appear to confirm the stricter mediaeval view of Aquinas rather than the late scholastic additions. It remains to apply the imposing edifice of historical and canonical teaching on usury to our present economic position. This is a task for economists who are also theologians.

APPENDIX 2

Trusteeship in Practice: * *A Wartime Experience*

The following account of the writer's experience (from 1940 to 1947) in creating and administering an agency for the procurement, rationing and distribution of newsprint for the entire British press, consisting of some fourteen hundred newspapers, has been added to illustrate the ideas in this book and to give some indication of their origin.

Admittedly, managerial experience in wartime cannot be translated directly into maxims or principles for peace. But this does not mean that there are not important lessons to be learnt in war that can help us see more clearly the objects of industrial policy and the means by which they may be realised in peace. Sir Oliver (later Lord) Franks's lectures delivered to the London School of Economics in 1947 and published under the title *Central Control and Planning in War and Peace*, have already been mentioned (page 32). Another example is that of Marshal Foch, whose *Principles of War* repeats one of the oldest expositions of the essentials of the art of management, summarised many years ago by Xenophon in the aphorism: 'The art of war is, in the last resort, the art of keeping one's freedom of action.'

On 29 April 1940 I was summoned to Stornoway House, Lord Beaverbrook's home overlooking St James's Park, and shown into a large sitting-room on the ground floor where I found Lord Beaverbrook and Lord Camrose. After a few preliminaries Lord Beaverbrook said:

> We want to borrow you for the duration of the war. You will be responsible to the newspaper proprietors and the British government for the supply, delivery and rationing of newsprint for the entire British press. All fourteen hundred newspapers will be in the scheme and it will

* This appendix should be read in conjunction with Chapter 10.

be financially underwritten by our joint and several guarantees. We want you to buy and operate a fleet of ships, set up the company, and devise a rationing scheme that is fair to all. We have agreed the plan with the war cabinet and our ships are to run free of control by the Ministry of War Transport, but in co-operation with them. Will you undertake this for us?

When replying, I did not know that the Newspaper Proprietors' Association and representatives of the Provincial Newspapers' Association were sitting together in a room upstairs waiting for my answer. That night I spoke to my principals, the International Paper Company in New York, and we agreed that everything would be accepted except a very substantial salary which they and I felt was unnecessary. Instead, I was to be loaned free of charge to the British press for the duration of the war.

It soon became apparent that this was a wise precaution. For although the press lords were unanimous in wanting to avoid government control, they were by no means agreed as to how to set up a supply organisation required to be 'fair to all'. Lord Beaverbrook, as we talked together during the next few days, came out with one or two strange ideas. He spoke of bringing paper to London and selling it to the newspapers from there as needed. This was impracticable and I told Lord Beaverbrook so. From that moment he treated me as a colleague and friend, promising to do whatever I asked, and was as good as his word. I was fortunate in having Lord Beaverbrook's constant agreement and support.

I had already resolved that our first step would be to require all newspapers to adopt standard reel sizes, so that wherever ships were able to make port the paper could be used locally. This would free shipping from the dangerous Channel route to London, and by using the ports of Liverpool and Glasgow we saved internal road and rail transport. The scheme was all but agreed when Major (later Col. Lord) Astor said *The Times* must be excluded. I told Lord Beaverbrook that it would cost only five thousand pounds to alter *The Times'* machinery and there and then we made an agreement with the Major.

We bought two Liberty ships in San Francisco, and they both arrived safely with cargoes of precious newsprint. We borrowed from International Paper and Associated Newspapers their paper-carrying ships, six in all, and this, together with two of Bowaters' fleet and three we subsequently built on Teeside and the Tyne, gave us a fleet of thirteen ships, of which four survived the war.

My lawyer was Tom, afterwards Sir Thomas, Overy. He, and Alan Welsford of Slaughter and May, helped set up the Newsprint Supply Company as a non-profit-making company limited by guarantee, with joint and several guarantees given by the press lords for a million pounds each. This permitted us to borrow the money we needed without further security. To buy ships, I had to raise an immediate loan by telephone of a million pounds from a London bank and when asked 'on what security?' replied 'on the security of the British press'. That was good enough.

We set up a Rationing Committee with Stanley Bell, the managing director of the *Daily Mail,* as chairman. It consisted of practical newspaper men, plus Sir Eric Bowater representing the home mills, and the paper controller. The board met every Friday at 11 am in the great boardroom at Reuters. The twelve directors included all the press lords: Beaverbrook (chairman), Rothermere (vice-chairman), Camrose, Southwood, Kemsley, Sir Walter (afterwards Lord) Layton and Major (Lord) Astor, plus John Scott of the *Guardian* and two representatives of the provincial press. They were in a state of such fierce competition that provided I explained in advance what was needed to the chairman and two or three of the other directors, it was usually enough to secure a majority at the board. Lord Beaverbrook presided but after he became Minister of Aircraft Production, Lord Rothermere took the chair. Lord Beaverbrook continued to lend his support throughout. I was alone with him a good deal during the first week of May 1940, and had the privilege of watching him manoeuvre Neville Chamberlain out of office and Winston Churchill in as Prime Minister. It was a fateful moment for Britain. During these negotiations I asked Max, 'What do you hope for yourself out of this?' to which Lord Beaverbrook replied 'I would like to be offered the Ministry of Agriculture; I have campaigned for British agriculture for ten years.' A few days later Churchill made Beaverbrook Minister of Aircraft Production, where his feverish energy and determination procured the aircraft which enabled us to fight and win the Battle of Britain that September (1940).

We were charged by the government with seeing that each newspaper received its fair share of newsprint at a price which was the same for everyone and resulted from averaging the home and overseas prices.

In hindsight the Newsprint Supply Company was a highly

successful experiment in trusteeship. Our authority was derived ultimately from the stress of war, but the British press accepted the need for discipline and created their own control organisation to protect their freedom. That was my task. Writing in his paper, the *Daily Telegraph,* on 12 March 1942, Lord Camrose described the company as 'a brilliant success', contrasting it with the French experience in which 'failure of the newspapers to perform their national duty had been frequently quoted as one of the decisive factors in the downfall of France.' The Newsprint Supply Company was, in Lord Camrose's words, 'a co-operative organisation working for the industry as a whole. It was not a profit-making enterprise.' All profit went to reduce the price of the raw material. As a co-operative organisation, the aim was to give every newspaper what belonged to it within the constraints of war. Our authority finally derived from the fact that we were attempting to pursue justice on behalf of all those concerned, including the reading public, the government, and the newspapers and their staffs. The company was organised as a 'responsible company' (the title of a book I afterwards wrote).[1]

The rationing system had to be complex in order to be fair. Every newspaper had a different requirement depending on its format, readership, advertising and market. Some groups had strong weekend papers, others depended on their morning and evening sales. We devised a system of alternative quotas based on use during one of two lengthy periods chosen at the newspaper's option. The quota could be used in any way the newspaper chose but solely by that newspaper. Some chose to maintain volume and reduce circulation, like *The Times.* Others chose to reduce volume and maintain circulation, but to drop one or more subsidiary titles. This gave newspapers the maximum liberty. Only a committee of practical newspapermen could have devised a system so delicately balanced under such difficult circumstances. Eventually the national newspapers were reduced to a single sheet of four pages each. Yet, to my knowledge, there was never an appeal from a decision of the Rationing Committee, although the Ministry of Supply with its statutory Paper Control was always available as a potential superior court. Their representative sat with the Rationing Committee and was kept informed of the company's activities. When, as occasionally happened, the committee reached an impasse and felt it could not solve the problem before it, the chairman, Stanley Bell, would let a pause intervene by adjourning the meeting for ten minutes. When we came back, he would invite the members to look at the position 'from the other end'. It usually led to an immediate solution. Without being conscious of it, we were adopting the ninth rule of the Natural Law which Thomas Hobbes put in this way: 'that a man imagine himself in the place of the party with whom he hath to do, and reciprocally him in his.'[2]

Each newspaper sent in to the company a weekly account of its consumption. The figures were checked in the office. One large provincial evening paper returned figures that looked wrong. We sent a staff member to inquire. He reported that false figures had been returned by which the paper in question had been able to increase its circulation by over one-third. The Rationing Committee was informed and a decision reached to require the paper to repay the whole of the over-consumption. It meant a fifty per cent cutback in circulation and a huge loss. I got wind of the fact that Sir Walter Layton, now chairman of the Rationing Committee, intended on his return to London to see the press lord concerned to 'work out a solution'. This signalled to me that the board were inclined to reprieve the newspaper, whose proprietor was a director of the Newsprint Supply Company. I immediately took a taxi to see the press lord and within minutes he had agreed, with grace, that to make an exception in the Rationing Committee rules for his newspaper would destroy the company's moral authority. On his return to London, Sir Walter accused me of going behind his back, but he generously forgave me, knowing that what was at stake was an issue of principle. Nothing would have destroyed confidence more quickly than a special concession made to a director. I suspect the whole of the Rationing Committee would have resigned if necessary, but fortunately it never came to that.

In a letter in *The Times* about this time I referred to the creation of the Newsprint Supply Company as the 'portent of a new social order'. Lord Beaverbrook replied next day saying it was a manifestation of capitalism. I think we were both right.

No newspaper failed to appear during the war through lack of newsprint. The Newsprint Supply Company enabled the British press to stay independent and intact by providing an instrument of self-administration with suitable safeguards on behalf of the community. A committee of the war cabinet, consisting of the Chancellor, the Minister of Production and the Minister of Information, was charged with the duty of overview. But in practice it met with us only rarely, for we had no dispute with the Ministry of Supply I can remember that was not resolved by the

Undersecretary, Sir William Palmer, who set an admirable example of working with the representative organs of the industry on a basis of trust rather than suspicion. Nevertheless, the safeguard for the public interest was there. I recall an occasion when the *Daily Worker* (the forerunner of the *Morning Star*) ran out of paper and appealed to us for help. None of the home mills would supply a newspaper whose credit they said was shaky but which was really regarded as a political risk. I decided we ought to go to the length of cutting sheets from reels to help keep the *Daily Worker* going, on the grounds that it was not the business of the press to censor a fellow newspaper but that of the government. So for a time the British press paid to keep a communist newspaper alive during the war. When the Home Secretary banned the *Daily Worker* for hindering the war effort, I felt we had remained faithful to our purpose, which was to supply and distribute the raw material to the whole press as efficiently as possible. An editorial of 28 June 1947 in *World's Press News* spoke of 'the high ideal represented by the Newsprint Supply Company'. In that year I went back to my own business and Patrick Bishop took over. (He later became Sir Patrick and an MP.)

The Newsprint Supply Company was conceived at a time of national emergency. But it was entirely managed by people concerned with their own interests in a highly competitive business. Thanks to a constitution which undertook to give the customer, the community and the industry a fair deal, supported by authority in the shape of a government referee (Sir William Palmer), the company proved so successful in practice that it continued to operate until 1959 when, there being no longer any need to ration newsprint, it was wound up.

This experience of creating and managing over a period of seven years, partly in war and partly in peace, a company required by the government to procure, ration and distribute the raw material of the British press, taught me the power of an idea when it is embodied in a suitable constitution. In retrospect, it seems astonishing that men like Lord Beaverbrook, Lord Rothermere and Lord Camrose, in matters concerning their closest business interests, for so long accepted the instructions of a small voluntary control body set up, it is true, partly by themselves but with no power of its own except the power of resignation. The steady pursuit of justice was, I think, the reason for the Newsprint Supply Company's success and for the fact that the authority of its management remained unquestioned.

NOTES

PREFACE

1. Sir Arthur Bryant: *English Saga (1840–1940)*, Collins and Eyre & Spottiswoode London, 1940, p. 329.
2. George Goyder: *The Responsible Company*, Blackwell, Oxford, 1961.

1. TOWARDS A FRESH PHILOSOPHY OF ENTERPRISE

1. Montesquieu: *The Spirit of the Laws,* Bk.3, ch.3.
2. Ibid., Bk.8, ch.2.
3. Sir Henry Maine: *Ancient Law*, John Murray, London, 1930, ch.1, p. 14.
4. Lord Eustace Percy: *The Unknown State*, Riddell Lecture for 1944.

2. MINIMISING THE HUMAN COST OF INDUSTRIALISM

1. Peter Laslett: *The World We Have Lost*, Methuen, London, 1973, p. 18.
2. J.L. & B. Hammond: *The Town Labourer*, Longmans Green, London, 3rd ed. 1918; *The Bleak Age*, Longmans Green, London, 1934.
3. George Eliot: *Felix Holt, The Radical*, Blackwood, Edinburgh, 1866, ch.30.
4. Adam Smith: *The Wealth of Nations*, ed. Cannan, Methuen, London, 1925, vol.1, p. 267.

3. THE METAMORPHOSIS OF THE COMPANY

1. Kenneth Galbraith: *American Capitalism*, Houghton Mifflin, The Riverside Press, 1952, p. 119.
2. C.A. Cooke: *Corporation, Trust and Company*, Manchester University Press, 1950, p. 39.
3. *The Times* Law Report for July 22nd 1947. ([1948] 1KB 116 at 122 CA.)
4. *Palmer's Company Law*, 17th ed. London, 1945, p. 45.
5. Peter Laslett: *The World We Have Lost*, p. 22.
6. Emile Durkheim: *Selected Writings*, ed. Anthony Giddens, Cambridge University Press, London, 1974, p. 17.
7. Royal Commission on the Distribution of Income and Wealth, CMND 6172, July 1975, para. 323.
8. Rockford College Institute: *Corporate Responsibility*, p. 11.

4. THE TRUE MEANING OF THE INVISIBLE HAND

1. Adam Smith: *The Wealth of Nations*, vol.1. p. 421.
2. John Ruskin: *Unto This Last*, Smith Elder, London, 1862, p. 104.
3. John Locke: *Two Treatises of Government*, Bk. 2, para. 135.
4. Thomas Hobbes: De Corpore Politico, London, 1650, p. 37, pt.2, ch.10, No.7.
5. Ibid., p. 191, pt. 1, ch.4, No.9.
6. Sir Frederick Pollock: *Essays in the Law*, Macmillan, London, 1922, p. 34.
7. Adam Smith: *The Theory of Moral Sentiments*, Pt.3, Sec.3, para.7 and Pt.2, Sec.2, ch.3, para.1.
8. See the essays by Hiroshi Mizuta and Nathan Rosenberg in *Essays on Adam Smith*, edited by Skinner & Wilson, Clarendon Press, Oxford, 1975.
9. Adam Smith: *The Wealth of Nations*, vol.1, p. 338.

5. THE SOURCES OF MANAGERIAL AUTHORITY

1. Chester Barnard: *The Functions of the Executive*, Harvard University Press, 1958, p. 170.
2. Sir Oliver Franks: *Central Planning & Control in War and Peace*, London School of Economics, 1947, p. 32.

6. THE CHALLENGE OF SOCIAL RESPONSIBILITY

1. Elton Mayo: *The Social Problems of an Industrial Civilisation*, Harvard University Press, 1954.
2. Paul Hill: *Towards a New Philosophy of Management*, Gower Press, London, 1971.
3. General Smuts: *Holism and Evolution*, Macmillan, London, 1926, p. 99.
4. Institute of Economic Affairs: *Lessons from Japan*, Hobart Paper No.58, 1947, p. 43.
5. C.C. Pocock: *More Jobs*, The Ashridge Lecture for 1977, p. 10.

7. FINDING AN AGREED OBJECTIVE

1. W.H. Beveridge: *Full Employment in a Free Society*, Allen & Unwin, London 1944, p. 47.
2. Ibid., p. 206.
3. George Goyder: *The Future of Private Enterprise*, Blackwell, Oxford, 1951, p. 1.
4. Confederation of British Industry: *The Responsibilities of the British Public Company*, 1973, para.23, p. 9.
5. British Institute of Management: *Towards Social Responsibility*, Survey Report 28, 1976.
6. Paul Hill: *Towards a New Philosophy of Management*, Gower Press, London, 1971, ch.4.

8. THE GENERAL PURPOSES CLAUSE

1. L.C.B. Gower: *Modern Company Law*, Stevens, London, 4th ed., 1979, ch.8.
2. British Institute of Management: *Towards Social Responsibility*, p. 55.
3. Fred Hirsch: *Social Limits to Growth*, Routledge, London, 1977, p. 179.
4. William Temple: *Christianity and Social Order*, Penguin, London, 1942, p. 57.
5. Peters and Waterman: *In Search of Excellence*, Harper, New York, 1982, p. xxii.
6. British Institute of Management: *Towards Social Responsibility*, pp. 39/41.

9. THE REDEMPTION OF EQUITY CAPITAL

1. R.H. Tawney: *An Introduction to a Discourse on Usury*, G. Bell & Son, London, 1925, p. 122.
2. J.M. Keynes: *The General Theory of Employment, Interest and Money*, Macmillan, London, 1973, vol.1, p. 351.
3. Adam Smith: *The Wealth of Nations*, vol.1, p. 338.
4. The Companies Act 1985, Sections 162/180.
5. Adam Smith *The Wealth of Nations*, vol.1, p. 420.

10. THE DIRECTORS AS TRUSTEES

1. Paul Hill: *Towards a New Philosophy of Management*, Gower Press, London, 1971, p. 198.
2. F.W. Maitland: *Selected Essays*, Cambridge University Press, 1936, p. 214.
3. C.A. Cooke: *Corporation, Trust and Company*, p. 75.
4. [1962] 2 All England 929.

11. MAKING EMPLOYEES SHAREHOLDERS

1. Richard Cockman: 'The Growth and Future of Employee Share Schemes', *National Westminster Bank Quarterly Review*, Aug. 1980, p. 51.
2. Simmons & Mares: *Working Together*, New York University Press, 1985, p. 136.
3. John Ruskin: *Unto This Last*, p. 102.

12. WIDENING THE ANNUAL GENERAL MEETING

1. Elton Mayo: *Human Problems of an Industrial Civilisation*, Macmillan, London, 1933, and *Social Problems of an Industrial Civilisation*.
2. Bakke: *Citizens Without Work*, Yale University Press, 1947.

13. THE SOCIAL AUDIT

1. *Social Responsibilities of Business*, Manaktalas, Bombay, 1966, p. 25/32.
2. *Social Audit*, Spring 1976, p. 90/91.

14. THE REFORM OF NATIONALISATION

1. Clegg and Chester: *The Future of Nationalisation*, Blackwell, Oxford, 1935, p. 146.
2. H.M. Stationery Office, HMSO HC 371, 1968.
3. D.H. Lawrence: *Phoenix* (The Posthumous Papers), 'Nottingham and Mining Countryside', Heinemann, London p. 138/139.

15. CREATIVE ENTERPRISE

1. Graham Bannock: *Lloyds Bank Review*, October 1981.
2. C.C. Pocock: *More Jobs* The Ashridge Lecture for 1977, p. 10.

APPENDIX 1

1. R.H. Tawney: *A Discourse Upon Usury*, G. Bell & Son, London, 1925, p. 171.

APPENDIX 2

1. George Goyder: *The Responsible Company*, Blackwell, Oxford, 1961.
2. Thomas Hobbes: *Elements of the Law*, Cambridge University Press, 1928, p. 71.

INDEX